LEGACY SPEAKS

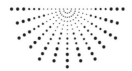

BRIDGET AILEEN SICSKO   ALIA MARIE SOBEL

ALLISON CANALES   ALYSEMARIE GALLAGHER WARREN

AMANDA RUMORE   ANNETTE MARIA

ASHLEY DUFRESNE   BRANDY KNIGHT   CAITLIN LYNCH

DANIELLE MASSI, MS, LMFT   GINA FRANCES

HAILEY PARKES   HEATHER ROBINSON

JANA BARTLETT ALONSO   JESSICA TORRES

JODIE STIRLING   JULIA RUGO

KATELYN ANNEMARIE BRUSH   LÍGIA LEITE

MEGAN KRAMER   MELISSA LAMBOUR

PATRICIA LAMBERT GENT   RACHEL SIMS

STEFANI SILVERMAN   STEPHANIE HEATH

TONI-ANN CAPECE

EXALTED PUBLISHING HOUSE

Copyright © 2021 by Exalted Publishing House and Bridget Aileen Sicsko

IBSN: 978-1-7371857-0-3

All rights reserved. Apart from any fair dealing for the purposes of research or private study, or criticism or review, as permitted under the Copyright, Designs, and Patents Act 1988, this publication may only be reproduced, stored, or transmitted, in any form or by any means, with the prior permission in writing of the copyright owner, or in the case of the reprographic reproduction in accordance with the terms of licensees issued by the Copyright Licensing Agency. Enquires concerning reproduction outside those terms should be sent to the publisher.

In loving memory of Mary Alice Shortall

CONTENTS

INTRODUCTION

To be honest, this book was birthed out of thoughts of death. In the months after my aunt's passing, I was brought face to face with grief, hidden emotions, happy memories and most importantly, questions.

In those moments, I was left thinking about the beautiful life she led, all those who she had helped and her devout connection with God.

Her death allowed me to ask some deeper questions:
"What will people say about me when I'm no longer earth side?"
"What will I leave behind?"
"Who will I have helped?"
"What will I have created?"
"How will people remember me?"

And thus, Legacy Speaks was born.

A collection of powerful, stunning, and emotionally-charged stories written by women who have a legacy to leave. They know they were born for a reason and understand that the events of their life paved the way for beauty, purpose, and legacy.

2021 is a time unlike anything we've experienced before. But more importantly, a time where women's voices are finally being heard, respected, and honored. This is a time in history where inspiring and empowering stories must be heard.

Allow these stories to remind you, the reader, that you too are never alone, and that whatever challenges you have endured, you too are here to leave a legacy.

What is your imprint on humanity?

Bridget Aileen Sicsko

ALIA MARIE SOBEL

TWO WORD STORY: REBEL SOUL

R. adiant
E. lated
B. alanced
E. mpowered
L. oved

SOUL

Before we begin, let's affirm together:
I am worthy of glowing radiance within & outside me.
I am worthy of feeling elated & the abundance it brings.
I am worthy of feeling balance in my life.
I am worthy of feeling empowered & beautiful.
I am worthy of loving myself wholly.

My life's two word mantra & legacy is REBEL SOUL. What even is a Rebel Soul? Do you want to know your Rebel Soul? The goal is to feel all that a Rebel Soul should feel on the daily.

THE CONCLUSION...

It took me to the age of forty to really understand what my legacy is. The legacy began at thirty-seven years old sharing Two Word Story —A Mindset Mantra I created. But as I shared, connecting deeper to my soul I realized, my legacy *is* a Two Word Mantra: Rebel Soul. You may wonder, "Why does she keep repeating those two words?" That's the thing; it's a mantra and meant to be repeated. You want to feel the essence of those words in your soul, in your mind, in your body. Allow it to fuel your highest good, your frequency of f*cking awesome, because we were born on this earth to feel AMAZING!!! But what happens as we grow up? As we start to "adult", things happen, our hearts get hurt, traumas show up and weaken our soul, dimming our light. So, this Two Word Mantra—Rebel Soul fuels me every day. It is my reminder that if I am not feeling radiant, elated, balanced, empowered, loved then I better check in with myself on why. By the end of this chapter, my hope is you will have a better understanding of how my personal trauma led me to discover my legacy and how it led me to my Rebel Soul. The unity of your Soul to your Mind & Body is the trifecta we are all *so* worthy of. It all starts with your Soul though. It is the root, where all peace, divinity, love lives.

Imagine a triangle. Maybe even grab a piece of paper and draw one. Within that triangle are beautiful radiant images of you, and on the top is the word 'Soul', the bottom right the word 'Body', the bottom left the word 'Mind'. And within the triangle are all the things that keep your Soul connected, strong and healthy.

I know I was born to share the message of self love and wholeness we should feel in life. So before I begin the story, I feel called to remind you, as you page through each of the beautiful stories in this novel, wherever you're at in your journey, your legacy exists. We all have one. Your Soul shares that wisdom with you. So keep going. You will discover the way just as we all have.

As I reflect on my journey, remember that our 'life happenings' can quiet our soul and make us feel lost, unsure, stuck, hurt, or curious what else there is to life. Do you ever have that feeling like something is missing? Or ever in a lack mindset? I did. And it really kicked with Motherhood. After my third pregnancy the feelings became so strong.

THE STORY...

Discovering my legacy started with postpartum in motherhood, crippling anxiety, deep depression, taking antidepressants all to become numb. My entrance into motherhood cracked me open and showed me what life was really about. I thought I knew before having babies, but boy, was I wrong. At twenty-eight years young, I had my first beautiful baby girl, Kylie. As I held her in my arms, all I felt was the greatest love I could ever know—but it was married to fear. Her labor was so taxing on my body, and I experienced a physical trauma I was not ready for. I was exhausted, in pain, and unsure how to navigate with this new human in my arms. I pushed through as women do and smiled through it all, not really knowing what was happening in my body energetically, emotionally, physically, mentally. So much love flooded my heart as we watched our baby girl grow, and at ten months old we made a big move from Chicago to Philadelphia. Happiness, home, family. I had what we so many strive for & dream of as little girls. Time went by, and when Kylie was sixteen months old, I was pregnant again! I felt so incredibly excited and ready to expand our family.

Until one day in deep winter, around eleven weeks in, I felt extreme sickness. Something was not right. My doctor hurried me in to find there was no heartbeat; I had lost the baby just before twelve weeks. The fetus was not leaving my body as a miscarriage would usually do, so I scheduled a D&E procedure at six a.m. to remove the fetus. Feelings crashed in. What did I do wrong? Why am I here? As I heard all my thoughts, a major snowstorm set in the night before my procedure with eighteen inches of snow. The trip to the hospital felt like the longest most difficult trip I ever made.

My body endured more physical trauma after this miscarriage. But I did what I knew to do, keep pushing forward. I did not acknowledge the feelings that were unaddressed inside me. Smiling, I was grateful for what I had in front of me. But the healing I needed to do was not at all complete. I had so much I left unaddressed but I had no idea how to address it. One year went by, and my next pregnancy came unexpectedly! At this point, fear riddled me. What if I lose this baby? Am I really ready to have another baby? How am I going to navigate this with my daughter Kylie's digestive health issues we had been faced with? Her digestive issues were so confusing and we frequented the GI Doctors at The Children's Hospital of Philadelphia. She had several ultrasounds of her intestines so that worry was sitting in my energy daily. My feelings of fear all came rushing back as I looked at the positive pregnancy test.

My journey of pregnancy and motherhood felt confusing, heavy, and exhausting. But a mother is not supposed to feel these feelings, so I smiled. I kept a brave face on, hugged my husband and October 2021 welcomed our sweet lil man, Charlie. This welcoming was a feeling of completion, happiness & joy. There it was! There were the feelings I was supposed to feel. A third pregnancy did add more physical trauma to my body then the sleep exhaustion set in & another cold winter. At two months old, Charlie tested positive for the flu with a fever of 104. Fear, fear, fear. So much fear that it triggered all the fear I had swept under the rug from my previous pregnancies. I was swallowed whole with worry.

We made it through his sickness, as I should have known we would, I did not have the trust I needed. And at this point the traumas from the past were stored in me, left unaddressed, the postpartum was too big for me. It had been slowly piling up all these years. Each pregnancy's unique challenges had swallowed me further. I did not know the feelings of worry, fear, and anxiety were something called "postpartum". I didn't feel depressed—so why would I seek treatment?

Who I was at my core was rocked after having my babies. I never fully recovered after each trauma my female body went through.

Labor is a beautiful thing but it is also very hard on a woman's body. The tough labor of my first, the even tougher miscarriage and surgery, a second labor, then a scary rush to the ER with my second child all stacked on top of me to take me down. The brave face was no longer there.

My days consisted of tears, mood swings, and lack of motivation. I am so thankful for a dear friend who said, "Have you seen a therapist?" Desperate, lost, and scared I took her advice and saw a therapist for the first time in my life. I cracked the door to my healing but it was only the beginning to a long long road ahead of antidepressants & anti-anxiety medication. In each session, I felt the therapy working, but there was always a lingering feeling of anxiety. Without knowing how to be an advocate for myself, I let fear lead me, and my dosage was continually increased so high that I felt numb.

My soul was no longer able to see, speak, feel. My marriage was shaken to an all-time low after mistakes I made: spending thousands of dollars to fill the void, and drinking late into the night until falling asleep on the kitchen floor. I was trying to numb the numbness. Thankfully, the Universe, my angels, spirit guides stepped in. During the week between Christmas and the New Year, I forgot to refill my antidepressant script and missed two days of meds. Pulling into the grocery store one afternoon, I felt literal brain zaps while sitting in my car and called my husband to tell him I felt off. That was my *moment*. The moment I cracked the door a bit more to my soul. I stopped taking all my meds and talked with my doctor. My mistake of missing my medication led me to my destiny. The Universe guided me to this point. To realize I had enough. I needed to face the traumas shadows within me, my scary truths I was harboring inside. And not on medicine. Just the raw, natural me.

THE LEGACY BEGINS...

Now I was able to feel so much, I started journaling. It was an eye-opening experience. Do you journal? It can be a time-consuming activity, but at the end of a longer journal entry, I titled the page "KEEP GOING". I then used that as my mantra the next day. I felt myself call upon those two words when negative self-talk and low feelings popped in. I continued this method of journaling and taking only two words to carry my mindset through the next day. I was finding my way back to *me*.

As the door to my soul opened, it allowed a fresh breeze to blow in and sparked a calling to creatively share this mantra method. I hopped on social media to share Two Word Story. I thought just maybe if it worked this well for me it could work for others too. I sat in my kitchen in a baseball cap for three hours re-recording my one minute blurb as to what this was, how it works, then added a few hashtags. I thought to myself, "what the heck am I doing?", but I pushed past myself and posted it. And the rest flows from this one moment back on October 22, 2018. I trusted my soul to shine with this 'something' I knew could be a whole lotta nothing. But the power behind what it did for my own trauma healing ushered me to share.

So my 'self salvage' journey included hundreds of therapy appointments, tons of journaling, mantras and a new found love for yoga. I realized I do love myself enough to work hard and save *me*! It was through yoga that the door to my soul was open even further. Adding yoga invited the connection of spirituality. Namaste. That word created so much peace in me. And the legacy continues.

Yes, I was lost, undeniably numb and was in search to find Alia. I was masked by medication and bad habits for so long, but with reflection, journaling, mantras, movement, I felt myself emerge stronger than ever before. The Rebel Soul was born as I learned more and more about what strengthens the soul. My journey expanded as I added more spirituality to my life. More abundance flowed into my world: Acupuncture, Reiki, Chakras, Yoga, Meditation, palo santo, sage, crystals, the moon, angel cards, angel numbers, my birth chart… as you can see the list is extensive. I was intrigued & energetically pulled to the healing that all these things provided my soul.

Every day, I would connect to different magic that helped quiet my ego. My ego liked to remind me of my past and all the mistakes I made. That inner critic voice said I am not capable; as I shared these tools and what I know my ego told me I am an imposter who does not know what she is talking about. I am just not good enough to do the work that I am doing. But it was through these spiritual self-care practices that I combat the inner critic, ego, and self-talk I heard so often. The AHA MOMENT flooded in. I am meant to share all that I had learned, because it became clear to me that my legacy and a core pillar of my existence was to be of service to the collective. I was meant to assist others on their healing journey, reconnect them to their soul, and help them find their purpose to confidently manifest the life they are so worthy of! You are so worthy!

As my legacy unfolded, I decided to earn my yoga and Reiki certifications. These courses brought me closer to my soul and inner wisdom. This mind, body, soul connection led me deeper into my legacy creating and sharing so much from my heart: mantra workshops, moon energy events with a focus on journaling, spiritual retreats restoring the soul energy, reiki healing sessions, mentoring women 1:1 on their Rebirth into 5D consciousness meeting their Rebel Soul, creating & becoming an author of the Rebel Soul Journal, and now co-authoring this incredible book.

So let this sink in... It is through connecting to my soul that I have learned my legacy. It is through selfcare & spiritual practices, facing the shadows within, and clearing energy you can strengthen your soul's voice. Traumas, sadness, anxiety, fear all interfere with our ability to hear our soul. A Rebel Soul knows the feeling of peace is not reachable without taking care of *you*. Staying connected to your inner strength. A way to always honor your beautiful soul is simply grab your journal and ask yourself, "How am I feeling? How is my connection to soul today? Is it strong or did the ego take over? What does my soul want to say?"

If your soul is unsure or feeling stuck, what are you doing to tap into the wisdom within, to *hear* your soul? We often hear, "All the answers are within you", and it may trigger an eye roll or maybe a feeling of frustration because you do not know what the answers are. But you will. I am here, empowered as ever from the healing I did for myself. I learned what I am meant to be doing. My legacy, my mission is to empower women, especially Mamas, to meet and honor their R.E.B.E.L. Soul. I help women rebelliously love themselves, confidently knowing what they have to do to feel R.E.B.E.L - Radiant. Elated. Balanced. Empowered. Loved. every single day. My legacy ignites the light, keeping that R.E.B.E.L Soul spark ablaze within you. So you can manifest the life you are SO worthy of!!

The legacy started with sharing Two Word Story mantras but it has expanded beyond that. I invite you to know your R.E.B.E.L Soul. Together we can heal the hurt, clear energy that is stuck within to find your soul and true essence. Everyone is worthy of feeling 5D consciousness, total bliss from within even through life's ups and downs.

In the spirit of sharing where the legacy started and where it has evolved to, I ask: what is your Two Word Story? What two word mantra will fuel you and remind you how incredibly amazing you are? This Two Word Story you choose focuses your intention for the day, the week, the month, the year, all of your life with just Two Words. It may only be Two Words, but this mantra method can set your mind ablaze with creativity, determination, and inspiration, to charge you with the positivity you need to make it through your day. This Two Word Story is one step in the right direction of intention, manifestation, ultimately connecting with your R.E.B.E.L Soul!

Once you determine that mantra share it with me!! Then consider next, what keeps your R.E.B.E.L Soul strong? Each and every soul is unique. What does your soul whisper? How would it feel to wake up every day Radiant, Elated, Balanced, Empowered, Loved? You can nurture your R.E.B.E.L Soul. This is a two word story in itself that has SO much meaning. Maybe you choose the mantra Rebel Soul. Know that when you are feeling low, you can repeat these two words to remind you to take action, do something that will revive your energy. Simply ask 'What does *my* Rebel Soul need!? Honor it!

I will always be here, that voice reminding you to take care of you! That the answers truly are inside of you. Happiness does not come from things outside of us but rather from within. You just need to name those things that fill your soul up. As you finish this chapter, I invite you to place both hands over your heart, close your eyes, take three slow inhales and exhales and listen to what your soul is saying. Then jot it down in your journal. Have that heart to heart conversation with yourself! As you release the words remember to trust, surrender, and flow. You can always make time for you, time for your R.E.B.E.L Soul.

ABOUT THE AUTHOR

ALIA MARIE SOBEL

Alia Sobel is the founder of Two Word Story, a Mindset Mantra & Rebel Soul way of living. She is many things because she has found that our soul thrives by continually learning, evolving, growing. Chitown girl living in Philly married 13 years, and a proud Mama, Yoga Teacher (the Classy Boujee Ratchet kind), Master Reiki Healer, Soul Intuitive, Mind Body Soul Wellness Mentor (aka Mindset Interrupter), & above all else, creator of Two Word Story.

Her mission is to empower women, especially Mamas, to honor their R.E.B.E.L. Soul and rebelliously love themselves to confidently feel REBEL: Radiant. Elated. Balanced. Empowered. Loved. Alia ignites the light, keeping the Rebel Soul spark ablaze within, manifesting the life we each are so worthy of! She holds space through 1:1 spiritual wellness mentorship, Rebel Soul master classes, Moon Manifesting workshops, and spiritual retreats.

Website: www.aliasobel.com
Instagram: www.instagram.com/twowordstory_mindsetmovement/
Facebook: www.facebook.com/AliaMuftiSobel

Rebel Soul Facebook Group -
www.facebook.com/groups/424653615528385/
Two Word Story Videocast-
https://m.youtube.com/channel/UCKjvZKHz7o3f18uqrbVYibA
Email: alia@aliasobel.com

2

ALLISON CANALES

THE ART OF BEING AN EMBODIED LEADER

PAUSE.

There are mentions of sexual abuse in my story. My invitation to you, beloved, while reading my words is grab a cup of tea, a pen, a piece of paper, a cozy blanket, breathe into your body, and pause as much as your heart may need to while reflecting on how my journey may connect with your own.

I avoided my body for as long as I could remember. Like a disease-infested home with caution tape, I stayed clear. I tried to run away from being close to it as much as possible through an endless list of avoiding habits: sex, drugs, eating disorders, drinking, and overworking.

It was a collapsing home whose foundation was rocky. The insides were moldy, and when you entered, it felt like something happened in there.

CHAIRS KNOCKED OVER.

Fingerprints that weren't mine lingered.

Broken windows.

Spider webs.

Echoes of unsaid and spoken no's that were heard and not acknowledged.

My body was a crime scene left unattended.

The sexual abuse I endured as a child felt like too much to face.

The story of my sexual abuse as a child was something I thought I could run from. If I put it in a neat little box packed it away in a secret spot in the attic where no one could find it, maybe one day I could forget it existed.

If I avoided the collapsing home, I could prevent the collapse; this is what I told myself to survive through life. But when your home is collapsing from the inside, and your body is the home, there's only so much running you can do until you are invited into the liberation of your healing.

For me, leading others led to me embodying my medicine; and embodiment led me to leadership. One without the other is hollow; and they are gatekeepers to each other. There's no substance residing without the symbiotic relationship of the two. I learned this lesson when I started scaling my business. Like many other leaders, I had bought into the myth that the only way to be successful was to force, hustle, chase vanity metrics, and follow the "rules" to success that have been laid out by other leaders, gurus, and voices other than my own.

I listened to these voices. The ones who told me that to be successful, I had to *be* a certain way; that valued doing and pushing more than trusting my own body's intuition.

That way of leading worked for a certain amount of time, like it usually does until it reaches an expiry date; what was once sweet starts to curdle. My body didn't have the capacity to keep up because it was never meant to keep up. It was designed to trust itself, which isn't possible when you're depending someone else's design.

I was attempting to keep up by searching outside myself for the answers to what it meant to be a leader, to be a business owner, and to be a successful woman.

I told myself when I reach x, I will feel successful.
When I reach y, I will take a break.
When I reach z, it will finally start to feel easier.

But it never felt easier.

Although for a time, the way I was leading and conducting my business seemed to work, it never felt entirely right; it felt out of alignment with who I was meant to be.

I overworked myself and suited up by *doing* everything as a way of wearing armour. Listening to the voices of what others told me to do was a shield because I could hide. I didn't have to be in my medicine when I was hiding behind someone else's idea of success.

I had started to believe that maybe I wasn't cut out to be a leader, perhaps I wasn't supposed to be successful, that success was hard, and that to be successful, you had to sacrifice your health and your own values.

At the start of my leadership journey as a business owner, medicine was always present. I had a sacred vision for how I wanted to have an impact on people, but that vision could only take me so far because I didn't fully own my medicine.

That's when I had to return to the collapsing home of my body; when my nervous system finally let out in a roaring exhale of, "I'm done running because I am so f*cking run-down."

Success is body language, and when the body is collapsing, the success we've created without a solid foundation in our bodies collapses as well. To ascend into the new paradigm, I needed to descend into myself. Instead of seeking out the answers to why I wasn't achieving success, I had to seek out the barriers in my body that weren't receiving success. I knew deep down that success, wealth, liberation was my birthright, but I couldn't "get" there because there was no "there"; I was the "there". The success I was chasing was a mirage disguised as a destination. Collapsing had a theme of descension, and descension held a theme of death.

The identity that I was clinging to of who I thought I needed to be in order to be a "good" leader had to die in order to be the leader I was born to be and lead the legacy I was born to lead. By dropping into my body, a sacred dialogue emerged, one that spoke of not needing to be good but needing to be me in consent with my body.

The business plan I had been following dissolved.
Healing became the business plan.
Embodiment became the business plan.
Energetic mastery became the business plan.
Rest became the business plan.

It all started in the body. The physical, emotional, energetic, and spiritual body.

What I was running from the whole time was the key to my liberation and a pathway for sustainable success.

Liberating myself as a leader started with the invitation to map out the dead zones in my body. My body held scar tissue on a cellular level. Even though I told stories of my trauma from my head, I never told them through my body, and those untold became a limiting cage. I had to go into the pain so that I could lead with the fullness of my medicine.

I had to see my body as a sacred space again. Even with broken glass, chairs knocked over, and fingerprints that weren't mine, I had to take claim of my home again. The pain cracked me open to breaking open the doors to my collapsing home, cleaning up broken glass and making it into jewelry, placing my hands where other fingerprints were to make it mine again, and placing flowers where cobwebs once wove; adorning a space that was always meant to be seen as art, even past its rubble.

I had to create new movements of how I was leading my body to create new movements in how I was leading my life. This started with seeing my body as art. Art isn't meant to be beautiful; it's meant to move you. It's meant to make you feel something. That something doesn't have to be light, bubbly, and pretty.

It's just meant to be.

I leaned into the curiosity of my emotions that had been tucked away in the attic of my mind. Could I play in the frequency of rage, grief, shame, fear and find ways to make it fuel me instead of swallowing me whole? In what ways does it desire to be expressed through the body?

PARADOX & POLARITY

Through this artistry, what was once dead came back to life. There was union forming between my light body and my dark body as I started to see that these emotions weren't even light or dark; they just were what they were. The mastery of them came with embodying their paradox and polarity.

I learned that there's a paradox in pain and pleasure and that they actually register very similarly in the body. Being an embodied leader meant embracing the polarity of my humanness and finding union in that polarity. Just like art, embodiment isn't about perfection and having it all together.

Our leadership is artistry through claiming our bodies in their full experience of the present moment. Through mastery of the present moment, we create the legacies we were born to leave on this earth. I accessed this mastery through being present with what was presenting itself to me in the moment.

LIBERATION

I stopped chasing for answers outside myself.
I was feeling bored in my business...

Where was I feeling bored in my body?
I was feeling resistant in my business…
Where was I feeling resistance in my body?
I didn't know which creative project to work on next…
What felt most alive in my body?

I was afraid of launching my new course…

I dropped into my body, let myself express the fear, found the spaces in my body that knew this course was going to amazing. I found the union in both emotions.

I was the key, and I was the gate.

I started to ask myself, that if my body is art and its expression is artistry in motion, and art isn't meant to be perfect, can I release the pressure for my leadership to be perfect?

Can I give myself the same permission to be as I give a painting? It's neither a bad nor a good painting. It's subjective; it's both / and.

Can I let myself be a masterpiece and a work in progress as a leader all at the same time?

Yes, and you can too, beloved.

When I came home to my embodiment, the limitations and barriers that prevented me from being successful dissolved. In order for me to lead with the fullness of my medicine, I had to be in alignment with my whole self-expression, which included both / and.

I didn't have to follow anyone else's rules to succeed; I created my own rules.

My expression didn't need to be perfect anymore; it just needed to be me, and that was more than enough.

The voices that told me to "keep up" in order to belong were no longer there, because I found belonging in my home, my body. Trying to "keep up" by overworking, grinding, and hustling at the expense of my values, my body, my health, and my expression was connected to the same energy of intrusion that had happened to me as a child. There was an authority that tried to override and take my power away, and I was conditioned to believe that gaining this power back would come from outside my body.

I gave myself permission to be with me and this is when I found liberation and freedom in how I lead. My expression wasn't meant to be palatable in perfectly curated Instagram posts that converted potential clients into clients. It didn't need to grab, pull, tug, convince anyone that I was worthy of buying from. Art isn't meant to be understood by the masses but by those who resonate with the frequency the art is emulating.

THE ART BODY

Your art body is a sacred expression and extension of God, the universe, Gaia, creator, anything you call it. There's nothing more perfect than your unique expression of artistry where you lead from in your own unique way. I started to see that I held power to receive all that I had desired just by being me.

I stopped putting my body through the performing and playing the part of what had seemed the most acceptable and loveable so I could belong.

I started playing for myself a solo performance where I was the artist, the muse, the creator, the audience, and gatekeeper to who gets to experience my energy.

We break the rules of leadership by creating new ways we lead ourselves. I had a sacred vision to heal the earth until I realized I didn't need to heal the earth; I needed to heal myself, and that's how I heal the earth. The new paradigm of business and leadership invites us to be in tune with ourselves so we can become in tune with the earth. We are extensions of her medicine. The earth doesn't judge itself for its cycles of the season's winter, spring, summer, and fall. They carry opposing yet symbiotic energy that creates synergy. Earth has its own blueprint for thriving; it knows this at its core, and within us, we have a blueprint to not just survive on this earth but to thrive. We are destined to lead radiant paths, and leading a radiant path isn't the absence of the darkness; it's embracing the full spectrum of our humanity and finding union in the both / and.

The more I choose my full self-expression in all of its polarity, the more that was also destined to come to me came with ease money, clients, and opportunities. I didn't need to try so hard or force success. Instead of seeing success as a destination, I became the embodiment of success in the present moment.

My legacy was created through being in the embodiment of my being in every moment.

I opened a channel within my body to receive all that I desired because I realized the "rule book" was never real all along.

My body that once felt lifeless and taken over by a trauma spell of sexual abuse throughout my childhood that led to more rapes as a young woman brought me closer to my aliveness. The dead zones were never dead; they were buzzing with dormant energy asking to be seen, heard, witnessed, and expressed. The tension in my aching heart and the heaviness in my womb were portals of prosperity when I saw them for what they were. Not wrong, not right, but the energy in motion that appeared to be dead because I hadn't seen the life force energy being held within them. These areas ask us to sink into our aliveness by bringing our attention to the areas that feel less lively, but in paradox, are the key to our radiance. We begin to integrate and weave together the both / and to give ourselves the permission we've been waiting for.

They show us where within us we are holding onto energy that constricts our natural flow of magic, we start to explore these areas, and we create a deeper channel for receiving.

We are born embodied. The journey home is to tell the stories of how we became disembodied through our expression. The more we do this, the more we create space to be clear channels for creativity to flow through us. We become earth warriors by opening our vessels for God's vision to move through us. We are muses, artists, Creatixes, performing for ourselves in connection to something bigger than ourselves. We surrender and relax into our magic when we learn to stay open in the paradox of pain and pleasure and find that they are one of the same frequency.

Our only job is to be a divine expression of ourselves. To create spaciousness in our bodies for medicine to come through. We are vessels of creation to see new earth emerge, and this is only done through the deepening into our being.

There's no five step plan to be you.
Because you aren't a human doing, you are a human being.
The art of being an embodied leader is through *being*.

Everything you desire to receive is created in your ability to receive within your body. If you want to hold the frequency of a deeper state of success and leadership, the invitation is to allow yourself to be more deeply held in the bigness of your embodied self.

If you hold a big vision, you must learn how to be held.

The female leaders that work with me tell me similar tales of looking outside themselves for answers. I see a theme of disconnect in their bodies, and they've each been told and conditioned to believe that the key is outside themselves. They feel like their vision is too big to hold, their expressions are too messy to lead with, that their voices are too much. They want to cling to the armour and shield of multi-step plans and tangible, logical strategies, when the best strategy is embodied in their DNA.

THE INVITATION

My invitation, if you resonate, is to take a pause to connect with your breath into your body.

This is a return to reclaim your sovereignty.

This is a return to be in consent with yourself so you can discern what the best move for you is in your unique way of leading.

This is a return to reclaim the codes of success that are only known to you in your relationship with God.

Thank you for being here.

If there's one thing I hope to leave you with, it's permission to expand into your most liberated self by letting go of the should's of who you think you need to be and reclaiming your artistry of who your soul was born to be.

Embodiment work is work without words because words cannot express all that we feel. But my prayer is that you feel the frequency of the medicine behind my words, and trust that your heart and soul weaved together any pieces that felt missing.

Thank you for your light.
Thank you for your darkness.
Thank you for your paradox and union.
Thank you for showing up and leaning in.

I see you.

Godspeed.

ABOUT THE AUTHOR
ALLISON CANALES

Allison Canales is an Embodied Leadership and Business Coach who guides female-bodied leaders, artists and visionaries to liberate themselves from cycles of self-sabotage, imposter syndrome, doubt, and overwhelm. Through a holistic approach to business and leadership in the new paradigm, her work supports women to align with their soul's destiny. Allison holds a sacred space to transcend trauma and activate womb wisdom. With this, she guides women to their sovereign feminine power so they may lead their lives and business with pleasure and ultimately magnetize themselves for sustainable prosperity and wealth. A catalyst for women to walk their most radiant path, to claim and receive all they desire in business, love and life, Allison is an artist, muse and empowered voice for new earth consciousness to come through.

Instagram: www.instagram.com/iamallisoncanales/

3

ALYSEMARIE GALLAGHER WARREN

YOU'RE INVITED

I want to start sharing this powerful journey by first calling in my team of light to be with you, sit with you as we journey. I understand that it's weird that I'm not calling them to be with me, but with you. I don't need to call them in, they are always with me. Let me share with you why that's true for me.

It's important that we go back to go forward. Let me set the scene for you. I'm around fifteen years old, I'm in my bedroom, the walls are pink, rose wall paper, clothes everywhere, bed never made, my journal never far away. My hair is long, I'm plus sized , and I've never felt "quite right" in my own skin. For a few years, maybe six-ish, I had been trying to figure out how to "fix me", or how to leave this world. On this particular night, I was ready to close my eyes and never wake up. I had been daydreaming of this moment for a while now—I was ready. I took more pills than anyone should, I lay down, and hoped…and I drifted off to sleep. When the early morning came, my eyes opened, and I felt fine. I was in my bedroom, I looked up at the ceiling and thought, "What the F&%#CK?" In a very clear and clairsentient way, I heard Jesus say to me, "It's not your time, you have a bigger purpose. Be my voice." I knew from that moment on, I was truly meant to share my story with anyone who was willing to listen. I always thought that it was my suicide story that I was meant to share, but now some twenty years later, I understand that it's so much more. That moment in my life is only one part of the story. The other part I recently realized was just how important my connection to higher powers would become.

It's been a long journey of trying to understand how this all works together. How all the puzzle pieces of my life will fit. It seemed like every day I would find another piece to the puzzle, and it didn't feel like any of the sides fit. But thankfully, I kept on trying, kept on picking up the pieces, and kept them safe—even if I forgot I had them. But honestly, the most important thing is to *remember*. The take-away from this little detour: stay on the journey, continue traveling, keep going forward.

No one ever truly has the answers for us because our truest answers come from inside. We already know our answers, our truth—it all comes back to remembering and waking up to ourselves. Our answers are in these moments, these memories, our puzzle pieces; that is where we find our truth, our purpose. This is where our answers are, inside us. Even when we understand this, we often deny it. Even when we see this truth, we look for different answers, different understanding—*other* people's understanding. We are told to look for a guru, or someone who follows an enlightenment journey. Someone who elevates themselves through devotion to spirituality and follows a path that sets them above others. But truly, the idea of a guru is another way we keep ourselves small or less than. We've been taught to mistrust our own knowing, mistrust our inner voice. Mistrust ourselves so much that we begin to believe that someone else has better answers for us, truer answers...*actual answers*.

We are taught that the guru must be outside us; it can't possibly be within us! We are taught that there is a path to enlightenment that only *some* people get to take, that there are chosen ones. We are taught that you have to be worthy, that you have to *work* to be worthy. We are taught that we are not innately worthy of enlightenment. *They are wrong.* We are born worthy, born a guru, born connected. Out of fear, the mindset shifted because how scary would it be if we were all our own gurus, *all worthy*, all the chosen ones, and put all on the same playing field?

This was part of the message Jesus was giving me in my moment, the message that *I was chosen*. That my story is my power, my voice is my gift, my words will heal. My words are healing *me*...my words will help you heal you. My words have the healing power of a guru. My words make me the guru I've always looked up to, the guru that felt a million miles away from me, even if somehow I understood that it lived in me.

Have you felt that before? Felt like something you knew lived inside you, and yet felt so far away? Have you ever wondered *why* it felt so far away? What was between you...separating you? *Why* was it separating you? What's standing in your way or blocking you? Did you build the walls? Did you lock yourself away? Did you build yourself the coziest room where you could feel safe and free, feeling small but comfortable, in a place you designed specifically to keep yourself small, safe, where you had no need to be brave?

This was my life, my story, and I claimed this every morning. I claimed my pain as a badge of honor because I didn't believe that I could possibly be worthy of anything else. The longer I walked this path, lived in my box, felt safe and comfortable, the more I knew I needed something else—something more. I knew I had a bigger purpose and that scared the absolute sh*t out of me! And, I had no idea how to live a different life, to claim a new life, or accept that life could possibly be anything else.

After endless nights of curling up in that big comfy bed of depression and doubt, I finally found my path, my people, my angels, and a way to break free, to undo everything I had built and truly find the me I was designed to be. When I stripped myself of the walls, the programs, the designs and beliefs, I was raw, bare, and ready. Ready to face the world, find my truest self; and I found her in the most vulnerable and unexpected place—the mirror.

I'm getting ahead of myself. I have to tell you that I've lost a child before. I had experienced the loss of something I wanted so deeply;

but this time was different. I remember this night like it was a movie I'd watched a million times and could recite each line by memory, but honestly it's a moment I never want to forget. I realized that I do not need to hold onto my pain and the loss of this child, because this time, in this moment of death, I was reborn. I was made new.

It had been about eight weeks since I knew I was pregnant. I was happy, and so excited to start our family in this unprecedented time of pandemic. It was all new but my child spirit was strong and constantly present in our space. I would see her in the house, in our arms, hear her laughing. But this night, things felt different, things felt peaceful. I was fully aware of what was about to happen. I woke up in the middle of the night, drew a bath, turned on the small heater in the bathroom, lit a candle, held crystals, called in Mary Magdalene, Mother Mary, Jesus, Archangel Michael, Archangel Raphael, my guides, multi-dimensional selves, team of light, and ancestors; I got comfortable and started saying goodbye to the tiny soul living inside me.

I cried, and cried until I couldn't cry anymore. I cried until I knew that what had needed to be released had let go. I was feeling at peace, knowing that She'd been earth-side as long as she needed, and she had already brought the gift she was meant to deliver. She had changed me, shifted me. She was preparing me for what was yet to come. But mostly her work had just begun, and in her death, she was breathing new life into me and trusting me to do the rest.

I sat in this moment for a long time, in the bloody waters of her death, of letting go, of saying goodbye, and embracing the love that can come from death. Her presence is still part of me and around me. As I became aware of everyone who had shown up in this night to help me shift to this new space of self-love, self-acceptance and awareness—to claim the space of my own beauty, power, and truth —she helped birth my inner guru.

It wasn't until the following morning that I really, truly understood what had happened to me in the wee hours of the morning. My mind had been occupied with how I was going to move forward after this, telling my husband and close friends, sharing the news that it wasn't our time yet.

But, as I was getting ready that morning to go about my day, I passed a mirror had to do a double take. It was like I was seeing myself for the first time. Like passing a stranger on the street and knowing that you know them. I stopped and stared at myself, in awe that there were no thoughts of doubt or self-deprecation. There was no self-hate or body shaming; only love. What I saw was pure beauty and love. I just stared and let my mind grasp what was happening, letting what had changed within me come to full realization. Stepping away from the mirror only to step back again, just to check and see if this was real and not just a dream.

I didn't think it was possible to feel happy that day, to feel love; I thought losing my child this time would break me. I had been so scared that I would crack and crumble under the grief of another loss, but it was exactly the opposite. I didn't crumble. Instead, there was strength and resolve, peace and understanding. I still don't have words to explain!

Some children come Earth-side just to feel unconditional love of a mother and leave before they are born because they got what they came for, but this precious child of mine, came to bring this gift to me. With the guiding grace of Mary Magdalene and Jesus, her tiny soul delivered what I needed to live my purpose...the *love* I needed to be my most authentic self, so that I could hold space for others to do the same, and prepare me to encourage others to seek and find the same love I am now living.

It has been almost a year since my sweet daughter crossed back to the other side. I still find myself checking the mirror to see if my beauty is still there, if I still see myself the same and feel the same as I did that morning. Thankfully, nearly every day it remains. When I can't see it, it's only temporary. This wasn't a band-aid fix like before, just patching things together until the real fix came along, or until I changed enough to truly see it. With her guidance, the love of Mary Magdalene, the protection of Archangel Michael, and the guiding light of Jesus, I found the beauty that everyone else had already seen in me—I found the purest form of lasting self-love.

That night I was invited to the table to sit with the angels and goddesses, to share the feast of life with those who saw the divine in me. It was then, at the table, that I truly understood the truth I was called to speak—the story of love.

This love wasn't separate from who I was. (Secret: it isn't separate from who you are either!) It wasn't a magic pill that I could take to make everything better. Self-love is a magic wand. The ability to wield the power to heal. This is what my work does; it guides you to find your own magic wand that guides the way. I am the guide, the channel, the funnel, but *you* are the driver.

In my work, everything I do is tailored to who you are and what you need, because healing isn't one size fits all. Healing is personal, gritty, and fluid. By making everything custom to the healing, I'm truly able to be the best healer I can be because I can hold space for you to be the best version of you. Just like in life, you have all the power, and I simply do what I do best: be the spiritual devil's advocate and ask you the questions to help you open doors, clear blocks, slay dragons, and fight demons.

This, my friends, is where the magic happens! When we fully realize we have always had all the power, always been the guru. Even if we need the help to wield it, feel it, and see it along the way, we know it's in us. When we feel the magic brewing within us, we allow ourselves to believe. When we see the magic in us, we allow ourselves to dream.

I am the mirror, the reflection, the pool of endless possibilities, and the scared safe place to speak. Speaking is vulnerable; speaking is real and grounded. When things are just thoughts, we can dismiss them or ignore them, but *words are reality*. When we open the door to reality, we need the mirrors to see the best parts of us. To see, feel, speak, and wield our love. This is the work—the truest, deepest, juiciest part of healing—in seeing our reflection, and not turning away from what we see, but rather cracking ourselves wide open and holding space with love.

Let Mary Magdalene and I show you the way, guide you, take the magic wand. You have been invited, you have been chosen to sit at the table and feast.

ABOUT THE AUTHOR
ALYSEMARIE GALLAGHER WARREN

AlyseMarie Warren is a Master healer, a healer for healers, and a guide. AlyseMarie has a unique method for awakening one's spirit to their truth as she leads them deeper into their remembering. In the process of healing, she is able to help individuals tap into their own inner voices, inner parts, and highest versions of themselves by guiding them to connect deeper within and to their wholeness. AlyseMarie's gifts are deeply rooted in divine love and her connection to Mary Magdalene and Mother Gaia, allowing them to come to her clients in a nurturing, loving, deeply grounded way. AlyseMarie uses a wide variety of methods spanning the quantum space, Acasma, guided meditations, painting, Reiki, crystal healing boards, oracle or tarot cards, and sound healing. AlyseMarie lives in Chicago in a cute eclectic bungalow with her artist husband, Spence, and their two cats, Kramer and Molly.

Website: www.channeledpathways.com
Instagram: www.instagram.com/ChanneledPathways

4

AMANDA RUMORE

EXPERIENCE AFTERGLOW

I t is July 29, 2018. I am nervously confident. Up until this moment, I never imagined I would be having an energy reading. Growing up Catholic, it was the expectation to shun energy-related work. I understood it as representing the Devil. Since becoming a mom in 2014, I especially try maintaining a distance from anything that could remotely offend God. However, today, I'm a media guest at Enchantment Resort in Sedona, where they specialize in new age spirituality. As I intend to write about my family's experience, I am offered a signature energy reading—and it piques my interest just enough.

I hastily walk through the grounds and gasp at the awe-inspiring beauty. I stop to consciously inhale the pure clean air and can almost taste the lavender growing nearby. The stately red rocks surround me while picturesque mountains are at my every side. To be here seems overwhelmingly magical. Not like witches and broomsticks; but viewing a vibrantly colorful sunrise while hearing a cardinal chirp a mesmerizing tune.

Mii Amo Spa is in my line of site. I progress ahead, and within a few minutes, I am sitting in the tranquil and earthy Mii Amo library, waiting for the Energy Guru. Earlier today, we met her while attending an outdoor family yoga class where she was also the instructor.

Kim soon walks in and sits across from me. She calmly begins, "We'll have an energy reading, perform an energy cleanse and have a second reading." She asks if I have experience with energy work. "I do yoga several times a week, love acupuncture, and I am completely mesmerized by energy," I explain, "But I've never had a reading or cleanse." I quickly add, "I will be writing about my experience for a magazine, so I will be taking notes."

"This treatment is designed to explore the body's energy and its innate intelligence. Energy work, meditation and breath work are customized to enhance your understanding and results," Kim continues. "Energy is our life source. We come here with a certain energy, and our energy continues as we move through life. Every person comes into the world to do something different."

Next, she suggests we move to the computer area. I sit and jot down a summary of her lessons:

- We omit fields of energy of up to three feet
- Color holds a frequency
- Chakras tell our story
- We hold vertical frequencies, vibration, color and sound
- We have 7 energy centers
- Our bodies never lie

Kim demonstrates how to use the computerized handprint. I set my hands down and see the colors slowly form as she explains that my aura is being read by advanced technology. The scan is complete, and she snaps a quick photo of my upper body. After explaining my aura, she looks to the photo that was taken minutes prior. Surrounded by white, she points to a blue energy. She suggests it appears to be a spirit holding my hand. I immediately feel a warm sensation run through body. Without hesitation, I know it is one of my grandmothers. Since their recent passing, I have felt the presence of both instrumental women.

Kim directs me through a beautiful energy cleanse involving smudging, meditation, visualization, essential oils and the sounds of gongs. After the cleansing we began the second energy reading. Kim points to a new energy color on my opposite side, suggesting I may have two energies along my side. I walk away feeling confident; I stretch my hands out, feeling the hands of both grandmothers nestled in my palms.

The next day is July 30, 2018, and we go on our planned family hike.

After navigating Boynton Canyon, a steep path with 250 feet of elevation and loose rock, *Kachina Woman* and *Warrior Man* appear in front of us. It feels like déjà vu, as I made this hike with my husband, Anthony and our four-year-old daughter, Mia Valentina, one year ago.

An infamous energy vortex, this exact spot is known as a spiritual location where energy is perfectly aligned to facilitate prayer, meditation and healing. Vortex sites are believed to have energy flow that exist beyond earth on multiple dimensions. Vortexes are said to have either masculine or feminine energies, but where we are has both. For me, that makes it extra magical and the ideal place for balancing energy within oneself and relationships.

I tell Anthony that I will hike *Warrior Man* first. Like last year, we will take turns climbing the vortex so the other can stay with Mia. Surprisingly, Anthony does not want me to climb. He is very vocal in asking me to stay grounded. I don't listen.

I don't remember much about the hike up. And nothing about the hike down. During my descent, my footing feels off. I scream down and ask if my foot looks secure.

What happens next will leave me with no memory for the next two weeks. I fall forty feet while hitting my head repeatedly on those infamous Red Rocks. I am broken and bloody. I do not remember my husband triaging me, but his practical military experience saves my life. While stopping my bleeding and attending to Mia, he fights with 9-1-1, making sure they send a helicopter for my body—I will not live any other way. Twice, Anthony and our daughter are told I will not make it. When they arrive at the Flagstaff hospital, he thinks I am in fact dead.

I am not conscious to hear these calls being made or the prayers being said. The drives that begin and flights being booked. My army is activated while my world continues to fight for my life.

I am alive but cannot walk, with a cracked vertebrae, broken arm and traumatic brain injury. My body cannot move for days while I recover in a Flagstaff hospital. But when Anthony plays Stevie Nicks for me from his smartphone, I move my toes trying to dance along. Gasps fly through the room—nobody can believe what is happening. Anthony films a video as a medical team teaches me how to walk; I'm sure it will be agonizing to watch back later. I tell everyone in Flagstaff that the spirits of my grandmothers saved me. I can visibly see them in the hallways and talk to them from my hospital room.

My first memory is around August 15, 2018. I am in an ambulance driving from Flagstaff to Scottsdale, which is closer to home. With my mom sitting near, I drift away. I am asleep through the usually scenic drive that was now filled with a dark and heavy rainfall.

I am with both grandmothers, Helen and Valentine. My great-grandma, Pearl, is also with us. They look younger than the last times I saw them, but then I was younger too at perhaps fifteen. I don't remember our conversation that day, but, of course, I do remember what they were wearing. I also remember Grandma Val saying, "Make sure all those bitches know I still look good." And if you knew Grandma Val, you would understand that loving remark.

After a few hours of driving through treacherous wind and rain, we arrive at Scottsdale Rehab Hospital and I come out of the memory of being with my grandmothers. Soon, my husband, daughter and dad come to visit, just as they had daily in Flagstaff.

My memories at the second hospital are muddled. A few new visitors come to see me. I see limited friends and my in-laws fly in. I have access to my cell phone, which is probably unfavorable. A few friends text, asking to visit, but I say no. Many moments through my recovery I am not Amanda Rumore; wife, mom and grown-up. I am Amanda Ghezzi, living in Illinois with my parents and siblings. At one point, I believe my mother is in fact my daughter's mom. How confusing is that? I cannot imagine seeing friends because I cannot understand who I am.

With my phone, I can read and listen to messages of great hope, often learning of prayer chains and prayer groups all over the country from Anthony's home state of New York to my hometown near Chicago and previous home in California. I am barely able to understand how this one act can motivate a community to come together in prayer. I am now living-proof that prayers are answered and miracles are possible, but it will take many months for me to absorb this evidence.

On August 21 , 2018 as I leave the hospital, I feel bewildered and scared. Even on the twenty-minute drive home, I partly expect to arrive at the house I lived in as a child. As Anthony navigates the way, we pull into our driveway, where Mia, my mother-in-law and father-in-law are waiting with signs to welcome me home. The hug I share with my four-year-old daughter is one of the best experiences of my life. Walking into my home, I feel happy and relieved. I know I am home.

It is crazy to see our ten-year-old pup, who was always near and dear to me, but will not come near me for three days. How can she not recognize me?

Although I had relearned to walk, being mobile feels unnatural. I have a step stool to reach my bed and a shower chair to bathe.

I am at the mercy of ongoing therapies, including physical, occupational, speech and psychiatric. Every day I am looking better but am suffering a great deal internally. I feel completely isolated, confused and fearful. Somehow, I fight aggressively forward, unconsciously determined to be a mom to Mia.

Most of these first days at home, I sleep and pray. I gaze at photos of my grandmothers; somehow, I know they saved me. Let's face it; 10% of humans survive a thirty-foot fall. I fell forty feet. 10% of humans that experience a traumatic brain injury can live a normal life. Somehow, today I am thriving. My body tumbled down jagged red rocks and landed between two sharp boulders. A few inched either way, I would have broken my neck. The science behind my fall offers such a small percentage of survival.

Fogginess and paranoia fill many days, which has led to weeks. I struggle to remember simple words, including colors or foods. But when Anthony plays music, I remember every word. From anything Stevie Nicks to Hypnotize by Biggie Smalls and Wonderwall by Oasis, music is what I remember most. And not new songs, but songs from my past. Music seems to be a catalyst to my recovery; the songs flow through my body, offering a glimmer of hope to the essence of Amanda.

My body tells me I need to be grounded. I try to mediate but it hurts my brain too much. I try yoga but I get too dizzy. I relearn the importance of breathing, and practice different breaths to affect my body differently.

While recovering, I acknowledge the signs I was receiving from the universe leading up to my trauma. I learn to forgive myself for missing the symbolism I could not yet understand.

In September 2018, I volunteer to read aloud to Mia's preschool class; at that time I have to fight to read a book. Surprisingly, in October I can drive! Even better, my husband surprises me with a shiny new car. I also begin to practice yoga with the instructor who had helped me fall in love with the philosophy. Soon, I start again as a lector at church, with enough confidence to read out loud to my entire congregation. After completing a task that was once simple, I feel proud. In November, my family flies to Italy to celebrate my first holiday season being alive! We share an incredible trip filled with new experiences, strengthening our family bond. In this time, it is increasingly obvious that I am suffering from post-traumatic stress and anxiety.

I start to write. My goal is to publish a book and fulfill that promise to God. I remember how to write, but now it's harder than ever. Words are often jumbled and my memories are difficult to recover. What will be valuable memories? Is it better to never remember? I am fearful and anxious.

As I write about my trauma and recovery, energy is a constant theme. After my first energy reading, I fall from an energy vortex. My survival makes no sense. I know God's grace saves me, but I also know my grandmothers play a significant role in my story. I am forced to believe and respect the correlation between God and religion with the universe and energy. I finally understand firsthand that these pillars of life work together in tandem, not in opposition.

In early 2020, my family attends a family party of a close friend. I am introduced to their sister, Bianca Jade, who is a professional intuitive and spiritual coach. We should have met previously since we live in the same town and have a similar tribe. The universe perfectly aligns our timing; I now need her guidance to further my work. Pre-trauma, I wouldn't have allowed myself the space for these beliefs.

When Bianca and I meet next, she uses her art to access my energy. She explains that my grandmothers did save me on that fateful day. Their spirits wrapped around my body to ensure my survival. This fall was my destiny and part of my plan before I ever walked this earth. I needed to rewire.

These words seep through to my core. I do not hesitate to accept this as fact. My mind, body and soul are aligned. I stop being angry and focus solely on gratitude. No more will I struggle with regret and remorse. On so many days of my journey, I promise God I will make him proud. However, on so many days my mind obsesses with questions. Why was I saved? What do I have to do to be worthy of life? What challenges will come to repay my debt?

Around this time, I become a part-time content writer at Tony Robbins & Dean Grazioso Mastermind. I love writing, and this was virtual with extremely limited hours. Learning about the clients and hearing their stories plus seeing firsthand the process behind Mastermind are brilliantly fascinating. Ultimately, I know I should have a similar path but don't take time to plan ahead. Although progressing forward with life, I struggle daily with TBI complications.

Completely content with my current workload, I coincidentally come across a job posting for a dream job. I haphazardly apply, not mentally in the market for such a job. However, in 2020, I enthusiastically became Head of Publicity at a national communications firm that focuses on clients making the world a better place. For the first time since leaving California, I am passionate about my work. This career move surprisingly makes me feel like the real Amanda. I find parts of me I didn't know were missing.

I have the chance to work with authors and coaches, hearing their stories often drives me back to my promise to God. A client who is a manifestation queen inspires me, and when I mention my mind can't manifest anymore, she eagerly teaches me how.

Simultaneously, I soon begin working on my legacy and call it Experience Afterglow. This title alone was a gift. One day at preschool pick-up, a fellow mom mentioned that my afterglow is noticeable. My presence on this earth is not unintentional. That conversation will forever stay with me.

Near that time, Grace, a dear high school friend and mom of two, loses her battle with colon cancer. In preparing for her own death, Grace personally wrote her funeral memorial and titled it "Afterglow". When seeing this, I know Afterglow is my life's eternal purpose.

As a TBI survivor, I may always struggle. But I also have an opportunity to teach through very personal experiences. I understand that energy is the foundation of life and it will beautifully coincide with religions around the globe. I have the ability to incorporate proficiencies from my perseverance, health, wellness, religion and spirituality into all of my work. My mission is to assist women in learning how to live life with God and universal energy.

ABOUT THE AUTHOR

AMANDA RUMORE

Amanda Rumore is a Spirituality Advocate, Speaker and Writer. She uses her profound experiences in perseverance, religion, and spirituality, plus health and wellness, to better cultivate her world. Amanda's mission is to assist women in connecting with their spiritual energy.

She has beat incredible odds and survived a harrowing traumatic brain injury. After plummeting 40-feet from an energy vortex in the Red Rocks of Sedona, AZ, Amanda teaches that energy is the foundation of life, and it can beautifully coincide with religions around the globe.

Originally from Chicago, Illinois, she studied at Arizona State University. Amanda then moved to Los Angeles and worked as a Hollywood publicist. She has since worked throughout the U.S. in entrepreneurship, public relations and media roles before settling back into the Phoenix-area as a wife and mom.

Amanda is determined to share her journey with the world.

Websites: www.AmandaRumore.com
www.ExperienceAfterglow.com

5

ANNETTE MARIA

COMING HOME TO THE FEMININE

Many think trauma is black and white. Cause & effect. In my experience, trauma has been pretty f*cking gray. This is my journey into my foggy gray healing and how you might walk the journey too.

Back in 2016, I moved home from university - back to the space that I felt unsafe for most of my life. Those years away had allowed me to experience discovery, exploration, and personal freedom. This had allowed me to create a sense of safety that I deeply craved for the first eighteen years of my existence.

With trauma, the mind may block out the memories until the nervous system feels safe and removed from the situation until healing becomes possible. This may include memories starting to flood back in, and was my experience exactly.

I started to have dream-like recollections of someone near and dear to my heart sexually touching me at a very young age. I would experience the memories yet talk myself out of its possibility.

"Why am I remembering this now?"
"This is fake."

"Maybe I'm remembering it wrong."

Doubt and shame flooded my psyche. But my body remembered. I would start to feel uncomfortable, unable to speak, and afraid to be alone with the person.

My narrative for close to two years became: "Annette, it's just a dream—that didn't happen." I was internally shaming myself for the experience.

Until I finally felt safe to reveal it to my partner, George, that I was sexually abused as a child.

With a heavy heart, I moved along my days; I was confused & my reality was shattered.

When we love the people in our lives as children, we trust them fully.

Now, I saw a monster instead of the person whom I had loved. I couldn't fathom how this had happened. The deep healing began when I decided to get honest with myself that this really did transpire.

From there, I spent weeks allowing myself to cry how deeply I wanted to. Screaming and releasing the rage of my innocence being taken from me. Loving my inner child in the way she needed to be loved, giving her what she needed at that moment. Grieving the sweet girl who didn't know what to do when her boundaries were crossed.

It was heavy. Moving through all of this was far from easy - especially because it shined light on why I acted the way I did as a young adult up until that point.

The sexual trauma didn't stop in my childhood.

When I first lost my virginity, it was through rape. I didn't even realize it happened until three years later. I heard a story of how Lena Dunham experienced rape, telling a story about being drunk and high and stumbling into a situation for which she did not give consent. A lightbulb went off, and I thought, "Sh*t, that happened to me."

I had been blackout drunk with no clear memory of the event, but for a moment towards the end when I begged to be taken home. The shame and guilt took over.

"Maybe you did ask for it."
"Well, you were blacked out. What did you expect to happen?"
"No one is going to believe you because you were so drunk."

The shame started to play a major role in my reality. I treated my body, my sweet feminine vessel, with the same emptiness that I had been treated with.

This energy of not valuing myself - and more importantly my Divine Feminine side—broke me.

My Divine Feminine was calling to me, "Take care of yourself. You are worthy to be loved, and you don't have to continue living as the little girl that was violated. You can change the narrative. Please honor me!"

But I didn't listen.

I kept pushing myself through the years, treating my sexual energy as an all-access pass. I worked really hard and never allowed myself to take a break or listen to my body.

My reality ran on unilluminated Divine Masculine energy. The Divine Feminine aspect of my soul left when she experienced the trauma, but she so desperately wanted to come back home. She was ready. But all I knew was to push through—to keep on keeping on. Because if I stopped, the hurt, shame, and pain would eat me alive.

I spent twenty-three years running, avoiding, and deflecting my shadow. That made it take total control over me and swallow me whole with crippling anxiety and perpetual burnout.

My body was stopping itself.

But then my Feminine made a final plea - "Please bring me back."

The Divine Feminine & Divine Masculine energies make up our realities.

The yin & the yang.

The sacred dance of energy within everything & everyone.

When we are disassociated from the Feminine side, a foundational piece of our energetic blueprint is missing. Our creativity is dried up, feeling at home in the body is a distant thought, and the connection to our vagina is numb. Dullness takes over.

Most women come from a space of unilluminated masculine energy for many reasons. Maybe they share my experience of sexual trauma, or have been told to put others first no matter what. Sometimes we don't value our cyclical nature or put worth into how much gets done.

The Divine Feminine not only called out to me - she is calling out to you. The energy of the Divine Feminine is rising on the planet. Mother Earth is calling out for us to hear the call from within so that we can care for her and others with deep love. But it begins inside. She deserves a space within your being. Without it, a part of ourselves is missing. When we feel like there is a void within, we fill it with external things, people, and experiences, unless we realize there needs to be another way.

When bringing back the Divine Feminine, it is important to note that there are two aspects of this energy: the unilluminated and illuminated sides. The shadow and light sides. The unilluminated side of the Feminine looks like overconsumption, stagnant stillness, and allowing emotions to run the show. While bringing the Divine Feminine back, it is important to focus on the illuminated side which brings an ability to flow with ease, create from a space of spaciousness, and trust one's intuition.

My journey of bringing my Feminine back home into my being in an illuminated way started small. I started to develop an accepting relationship with my physical body, and I started to see the beauty that is my vagina and sexual expression. Once I felt connected to my body, I was able to understand the magic of embodying emotions rather than suppressing them.

For the type-A woman that I am finding space to be, it still can be an internal battle. I try to allow myself time to play and create just for fun. To paint. To play with dirt. To dance. To create music. To write. Not for any specific reason, but just because it is important to feel expressed. Shifting my values to finding value in creativity just as much as working.

But my Divine Feminine not only needed care to bring it back into a healthy, embodied space. My Divine Masculine side was also too far on the unilluminated side, where my shadow side of not keeping boundaries, doing too much, and burning out still needed to be addressed. The unilluminated side isn't "bad", but it is a place in which one cannot operate from for too long. It is a great teacher with its own medicine, but staying there takes us too far to one end of the polarity. The balancing side is the illuminated Masculine where we are able to hold strong boundaries, create structures around doing, and hold our vision.

When we spend too much time in any polarity, we are unable to see clearly and feel the present moment.

Part of my healing with the Divine Masculine was to create boundaries & honor them. One of the boundaries I needed to create was with sex. My vagina was calling out for healing on an even deeper level. It called to me to reclaim my virginity, my innocence that had been taken. I needed to speak up with vulnerability and honesty to my partner that I needed to withhold sex to heal and spend my energy on myself. I was breathtakingly held by my masculine counterpart in this decision. 2021, years after I was raped, was the year I lost my virginity in the way that I wanted to.

And it was to the man I loved, with consent and memory of the entire experience. Afterwards, I wept from the beauty of being treated with respect.

After years of healing and intention, I am now able to integrate my Divine Feminine and Divine Masculine in an illuminated way. Finding balance within these two energies. But it is a sacred dance between the two energies that requires understanding of how to witness and shine awareness when we have gone too far to one side.

This gives us the grace to find a sense of harmony. It's not about being perfectly balanced all the time. It's about coming into an understanding of your energetic blueprint. The Divine Feminine and Divine Masculine can both be unilluminated or illuminated, holding their shadow and light sides.

Once you create this understanding and have the tools to bring you into harmony—you are an unstoppable, limitless and embodied being. Because you are no longer hiding a part of yourself. You no longer are looking outside of yourself for the answers because you hold the key to creating your dream reality.

My legacy with all that I do is for others to feel wildly expressed in living out their soul's mission on this planet. Because no matter that pain, trauma or limitations you have experienced—those don't define you.

You have the power to rewrite your story.

You have the infinite ability to co-create a magical future.

It all begins with you committing to getting to know all of yourself. To become radically honest with who you are and who you desire to be. After all we spend too little time working on our personal relationship. It's time for you to become your own best lover.

It all begins here, within you.

When you make the commitment to meet yourself where you are, you will find all that you may be seeking.

What will you choose?

You are the only one standing in your way. How liberating and how frustrating that is! The medicine lays right where the poison is.

Spending time working on yourself is the most impactful aspect of your legacy on this planet because it ripples out to all those around you. Showing others what may be possible in their reality. Rewriting history & redefining the future.

The work I do is to empower women to live out their soul's unique mission on this planet. No matter how big or wild the dream, maybe it was given to you because you are meant to birth it. The medicine is in knowing you have the choice within every moment to choose a new path. Just because you have gone through trauma, hardship, and "failures"—I don't believe in failing—doesn't mean you are unable to do what you desire

Oftentimes your ego will keep you contracted. Limiting beliefs will peek their heads up to keep you small, because the ego wants to feel safe.

Through working with me, I aid you in finding safety in expanding. In leaning into the unknown. In opening up to being guided to live out a soul-led life.

I firmly believe the more people there are living out their specific mission on this planet, the more harmony we will experience as a Collective. Because when you are on purpose, you are fulfilled and challenged. You are evolving into new levels of self, and no longer wasting your time and energy on what doesn't matter to you.

The old paradigm of struggle and comparison can melt away because joy and abundance is the new reality. We not only co-create our personal reality, we co-create the Collective reality. The more individuals that chose joy and abundance, the more that we can all experience.

Through supporting me, you also support the ultimate aspect of my legacy to create a retreat center and community living space in

Vermont that supports individuals in living out their specific zone of genius, while coming together for healing, possibilities, and creating ripples of goodness out into the world.

When we shift our perspective from me to we, magic starts to happen. We start to feel the ability that we are not alone and are able to reach new heights as a Collective.

Your soul has incarnated into this planet to live out a specific mission, to support this thread of oneness that is within us all. Part of your human experience is to answer the call. To lean into the discomfort and grow into your ultimate potential.

What will you choose? I invite you to know it is safe to come home to the Feminine. Your legacy is waiting for you to be birthed.

ABOUT THE AUTHOR

ANNETTE MARIA

Annette Maria is a Purpose Embodiment Coach, Intuitive Facilitator of Healing, channel for multi-dimensional beings, Bhakti yogi, and the host of Sacred Dance podcast. Her work supports women to step into their soul's purpose, reclaim their inner goddess, and manifest their deepest desires. She wants to see the planet as a place that supports everyone to feel wildly expressed in their soul's purpose, reminded of their limitless potential, and able to fully feel their humanness. She resides in New Jersey with her artist partner, George, and rescue dog, Max.

Website: Activationsbyannette.com
Instagram: www.instagram.com/its.annettemaria/
Facebook: www.facebook.com/annettemaria123
Facebook Group: www.facebook.com/groups/ShaktiRisingCollective
Insight Timer: www.insig.ht/annette.activator
Sacred Dance Podcast: www.anchor.fm/annette-maria
Email: hello@activationsbyannette.com

6

ASHLEY DUFRESNE

EMPOWERING THE EMPATH TO SOUL-LED LEGACY

D ear sensitive soul,
If you know you're destined for something greater and desire to lead your legacy from the core of your essence, this story is for you. This is a story about 'gut feeling' and intuition. That inner knowing; the language and guidance of your soul.

It may feel natural for you to follow this guidance, this gut feeling, but what happens when the pressure is on? How clear and confident are you when you have an emotional attachment to the outcome? How about something as big as your purpose or your legacy?

Things might become hazy, doubt may kick in, or you may become frozen by the fear of making the "wrong" move. You may start questioning yourself and your abilities. You may even circle around the idea that your soul has abandoned you in your most dire time of need.

But in those challenging times when you forget your power, purpose, and potential, you don't lose connection to your soul. Instead, you're unable to trust its guidance or hear it over the fear and roars of your ego screaming as it begs you to stay small in the confines of your comfort zone where it's safe.

Even though the Ego can feel like an enemy, the Ego is neither bad nor should it be "killed". It's an important part of being human, and no matter how intuitive or spiritually ascended you are, the Ego is there. As an empath, when it comes to things of great importance to us like our purpose or our legacy, even the most powerful and experienced channels can feel like a Muggle. Maybe you feel this way too? If so, I am thrilled to share my story and guide you on a journey to rise and lead your soul-led legacy.

The journey begins with little Ashley. She was a kid who navigated her life from trauma responses and conditioned survival mechanisms with her supernatural experiences and empathic sensitivities.

Picture this: a small, meek, little Ashley, weighed down by a compulsive need to control her environment. If she could not grasp control, she was met with a tidal wave of anxiety, panic attacks, obsessive thought loops, and impending doom that felt impossible to climb out of.

As a survivor of trauma, mental health neglect, and being a highly sensitive empath, the way I experienced the world was very different from those around me. Throw in my gift of mediumship and channeling and you've got a perfectly scripted horror movie just waiting to be turned into a Netflix special, which I was living out daily.

Experiencing reality differently set me up to be gaslighted by others often. As empaths, we find that others may not understand us or our experiences. Years of this taught me that I couldn't trust myself or my experience. I couldn't trust my thoughts or emotions, my body or that gut feeling I had that I now know as intuition.

To make up for this, I leaned into my Type A Virgo, "control freak" programming. I sought comfort in the finite, evidence-based answers. Anything that didn't provide structure or support would send me into a tailspin. Self-medicating and substance abuse were byproducts of my need to control and find temporary relief from my reality.

How I was living was unsustainable. At nineteen, it triggered a huge life-altering wake-up call and the start of my healing journey. At this time, I was able to rebuild trust in myself and my emotional experience. I became certain in my intuition and my gift of channeling, and taught myself how to confidently make decisions from my soul. When it came to my purpose, things were different. I knew the impact I wanted to make from a young age but I was still in the dark about how to lead it. I believe that awakening this wisdom in my childhood when I had such disbelief in myself is why I approached this with hypervigilance and control. It felt like the most significant part of my existence! I navigated my soul journey with a rational, logical mind because leading my purpose with my soul felt unsafe.

This looked like getting a degree in psychology and working in clinical mental health and therapeutic institutions. Staying tucked in the confines of science to help others felt like a logical approach. Even so, the nagging feeling in my gut made it clear something was missing.

That scratching at your gut is your
soul telling you it's hungry for more out of life.

The journey to leading my purpose was a slow one as I worked into feeling safe and confident in my sacred spiritual gifts. Yet, what woke me up out of wavering and into action was quick and harsh!

An Ayahuasca Ceremony in 2017 acted as a swift catalyst for me.

At this point, I had been offering Reiki sessions for five years, and in the last year I had been offering my gifts through energy alchemy and life-purpose focused channeling sessions. I loved these sessions! Seeing the profound shifts clients were able to make in such a short time lit me up. But, deep down, my soul yearned for more.

At this time, I was surrounded by spiritually gifted leaders who had their own businesses where they shared their unique medicine. I had the honor of channeling and supporting each of them in awakening their spiritual gifts, starting their purpose-driven business, or refining their life's work. As much as I was a guide on their journey, they were mine. They invited me to join them in Ceremony.

Ayahuasca acted as a much-needed kick in the booty and sent me on a path of massive life change—although not in an "eyes wide open to all the beauty of life" kind of way. Truth be told, my Ayahuasca experience was awful and traumatic (as I think it can be for many). I still joke to this day about resenting Mama Aya, but I know deep down that she was the medicine I needed to catalyze me into motion.

To save you a long, agonizing story, I'll sum it up by sharing the impression and lesson. I experienced a spiritual death without a second ceremony to fulfill my rebirth. Without that rebirth, I was left feeling empty. The emptiness brought me back to a familiar emotionally and mentally dark period in my life which ignited my inner warrior to rise up. I knew it was time to release the safe and familiar, and change.

The day I returned home, I ended my lease, quit my job, and planned my great escape. It was the beginning of my journey toward the highest expression of my purpose and legacy. This journey took me to the most isolated chain of islands of Hawaii, where I had no home, no job, no community, and most importantly, no backup plan or easy way out. Though I had been taking leaps of faith and honoring my soul's calling for years, I didn't foresee the depth of resistance that was dwelling within me.

You could identify this resistance as limiting beliefs or old, untrue stories, but what held me back the most was the trauma from being gaslighted. It made me feel unsafe and unable to be fully on board with my soul, and made leading with my soul feel unwise. Ultimately, it was traumatizing for me to physically take this soul-guided action when I wasn't emotionally all-in.

I had a history of taking these kinds of courageous (read: unthoughtful and reckless) leaps. This lack of gentleness and extremist approach to healing was a theme of mine that made my past therapist cringe. I approached my healing with brute force by pushing myself to extremes.

For example, in my early twenties, I witnessed that I was terrified of heights and large bodies of water. So, I decided to push myself to the furthest edge and go cliff jumping at night, completely naked, to push myself beyond the brink of fear in order to "overcome it". This, as you can imagine, did not help my fear and was not a very trauma-informed or conscious approach to healing. It's taken me years to heal that self-generated trauma, and I still can't go cliff jumping.

This move to Hawaii felt like that cliff jump, except the terror didn't end three seconds later when I plummeted into the water. It felt like months of torture.

A week before I headed to Hawaii, I went to a sound healing event where I had a profound vision. The Goddess Pele, who resides on the Big Island of Hawaii, came to me. I was in a cave, blinded and in a panic due to the darkness, I heard the whispers of Pele say, "You are completely guided, even if you don't see any more than the step ahead of you." As I relaxed and surrendered, a flame shone a light on my next foot placement, but no further. The vision continued in this way: panic, remembrance, surrender, then illumination. This foreshadowed what I was about to undergo on my journey.

When I arrived on the island of Hawaii, it was as if I was living the vision I saw weeks before. The complete unknown triggered an old trauma response of neurotic control and ego-led living. It was clear I was not on a journey of rainbows and butterflies.

Surrendering backed with trust is like leaping off the edge and knowing the net will appear. Surrendering without trust feels like falling off the edge preparing to hit the bottom.

I was standing on the Root Chakra of the Earth, and yet I was so disconnected from my own foundation. For the first couple of months, I floated in this space of the in-between. I was open to following the channeled guidance, but I wasn't in a mental, emotional, or energetic space to be able to receive it. Each day felt like an eternity of uncertainty. Eventually, I found a spot to pitch a tent on a friend's land in exchange for working on it. I was isolated and had limited resources without any clue as to what to do next. I cried out for guidance but was only ever provided with enough to make it through the night. Forced into survival mode, I became more and more disconnected from the possibilities beyond my ego's limited tunnel vision. I felt hopelessly separated from my soul and spirit.

Had I gotten the message wrong? Was I not supposed to come out to Hawaii? I didn't understand. I had been following my soul's guidance, so why wasn't it working? Why did it feel as though the Universe had turned its back on me?

The vision from Pele resurfaced, and I knew all I had to do was surrender. I thought I had been surrendering, but I was just dissociating. Dissociating is not the same as surrendering. One is a fear and trauma-based reaction while the other is a faith-based response. Truthfully, I couldn't surrender any more in this state even if I had wanted to. I couldn't because I lost my faith. I didn't trust myself, my intuition, my soul's guidance, or the Universe. I became bitter and resentful. How could I possibly live out my soul's purpose and take my business to its fullest expression if I wasn't supported beyond the bare minimum of survival?

To feel freedom is to feel open; to be open, you must surrender; to surrender, you must feel safe.

I knew something had to give, and with nothing left to lose, I released the requirement to rely only on myself and my channeling. I relieved myself of needing to focus on building my business and actualizing my legacy so that I could put that focus and energy back on myself. *It's easy for empaths to neglect themselves and focus solely on serving others through a mission-focused life.*

There it was...

Releasing the pressure created a minuscule amount of space for self-compassion to enter, which I sorely needed. It was then that I was able to finally loosen my grip on control, and as I did so, the blinders that had kept me stuck in tunnel vision came down too. The things I was once blind to became clear as day. It was like I had been living with darkly, ironic-tinted glasses...or living out a really bad psychedelic trip.

I didn't realize at the time, but those blinders were lined and reinforced with two *huge* narratives that had orchestrated this entire experience. The first was an old story of visibility equating to danger. Isolating on the farm in Hawaii kept me safe from the possibility of being seen making a fool of myself if I failed. The second was an old limiting belief around success. To be worthy of success, I need to earn it by suffering, struggling, and working excruciatingly hard. No wonder I found myself working on the farmland, alone and barely getting by.

With my vision clarified, I reached out to a friend on the other side of the island and was offered a place to stay. Even though it was temporary, I had food, water, and the support of a lovely friend. Most importantly, I had the capacity to implement some basic self-care. This allowed me to regulate my nervous system and feel grounded and safe enough to move beyond survival mode. My Root Chakra was finally given the love and support it needed. In this space, I was able to rebuild confidence in my soul, and loosen my ego's grip on control. As I did, more opportunities began to arrive in my life to support me.

I carved out time to prioritize whole-self reclamation; this looked like implementing daily embodiment practices that reinforced feeling safe and supported and helped to reestablish my divine connection. It was in this work that I came back to full trust in myself, my intuition, and the Universe.

These sacred steps allowed me to expand my energetic capacity to eventually find a home of my own where I would continue to nurture and grow my energetic roots for the remainder of my time in Hawaii. A few months later, the earth began to shake as the volcano twenty miles away from my home erupted. Because my Root Chakra was securely anchored, as the volcano opened up and birthed new land, my Crown Chakra mirrored its flow.

At last, I had finally reached the rebirth I had been yearning for months since Mama Aya. After the work I had done to anchor my roots, my channel had become clear and ready for a massive next level awakening. Within twenty-four hours of the volcano erupting, I received a substantial Intuitive Channel activation, and channeled in my first two courses. Within a couple of months, I channeled in one of my signature mentorship programs—Activate Your Life's Purpose—that is still changing the lives of empaths and spiritual entrepreneurs many years later.

I now have the honor and pleasure of living out the highest expression of my life's purpose as I lead empathic, spiritually sensitive leaders to discover and live out their purpose with ease and flow.

We are meant to feel lit up by living out the fullest expression of our purpose; but we cannot do that if we are swirling in doubt or trapped in survival mode. It's my greatest pleasure to guide sensitive, intuitive leaders in the process to unwavering trust in their divine power, their intuitive channel, and their fullest potential. I guide them from "soul's yearning" to discovering their life's purpose, feeling capable and worthy of it, and confidently live it out. This is my legacy; to guide sensitive leaders to lead their purpose from their soul, with the utmost fulfillment and joy in the process!

You were born to live out the most joyous and fulfilling version of your life imaginable—if you have a gut feeling that is telling you to rise into more, listen intently and use it as your compass. That feeling, that guidance, is in you for a reason. Ensure your whole-self is on board, and then open yourself up to receive it and the endless possibilities available to you.

TIPS FOR LIVING A SOUL-LED LEGACY:

(1) Instill Unwavering Trust
Trust is the core of your foundation, also known as your Root Chakra and your nervous system. It is in these systems that we cultivate a sense of security and trust. If those needs aren't being met, we can't access the higher expression of ourselves or our purpose.

Remember, you cannot fully surrender without unwavering trust (faith) in yourself and the Universe. It is unkind and traumatic to leap without trusting that the net will appear.

(2) Retrain Yourself to Believe in YOU
Developing unwavering belief in yourself is an extra process for empaths, as they usually have years of empath trauma such as gaslighting which has led them to believe they can't trust themselves,

their experiences, or their intuition. Reprogram your trust and belief in yourself so you can take aligned action with confidence.

(3) Remove the Blinders

What is keeping your Ego in the control seat? Give yourself the space to witness what's holding you back from living out your soul-led legacy. Witness the stories, debunk those beliefs, and rewrite them as your higher truth.

(4) Small Steps Create Positive Sustainable Change

Bigger isn't always better. Big steps won't speed up your timeline of living out your purpose. Instead, it can trigger trauma responses and dysregulate your nervous system, spiraling you into old programming as it did for me. Get clear on your vision, back it with your unwavering "why", and then take small, incremental steps that push your comfort zone but don't push you off the edge. Be kind to yourself, go after your purpose with all you've got, and do it in a way that isn't abrupt and traumatic, but instead, feels good and exciting.

ABOUT THE AUTHOR

ASHLEY DUFRESNE

CEO of Authentic Embodiment, Ashley DuFresne, is a Master Channel, Energy Alchemist, and Business Energetics Mentor who blends spirituality with her formal background of psychology to help Empath entrepreneurs and leaders gain clarity and confidently rise into the highest expression of their purpose and life.

Ashley guides her clients in leading their legacy and creating success with ease and flow within their life's work through understanding and honing their unique energetic signature and mastering their gift of channeling.

Her workshops, masterclass series, and signature programs, Activate Your Life's Purpose and The Purpose Accelerator Mastermind, have helped thousands across the globe.

Off duty, you can find Ashley scaling mountains in Golden, CO, studying sacred sexual empowerment, and taking her cat, Ulu, on walks.

Website: www.ashleydufresne.com
Instagram: www.instagram.com/ashley.dufresne
Email: ashley@ashleydufresne.com

7

BRANDY KNIGHT

THIS IS A LOVE STORY

I was always aware, even as a very young child, of the subtle communication of nature and how plants communicate to one another and everything else. I knew of the Deva realm: the all that is was thick and rich and all around. My heart longed and swooned in response to this from as early as I can remember. Goosebumps ran up and down my body as the less dense magical frequencies said "yes" to what I was perceiving. I commanded eye contact by those I recognized as soul family. Communicating telepathically more frequently than verbally. At that young age, I was also filled with the question of, "Who can I tell? Who can I share this with that will believe me and not brush it off as make believe?" Funny, that phrase "make-believe". As I grew, I learned how misunderstood those words were when used together. We quite literally make things by believing them.

I get a giggle visualizing my decision to come to this planet in this particular genetic line. This emotionally repressed lineage I chose to plop down into had seen generations of tightly-held survival mode. Like many family lines on planet Earth, healthy nurturing, physical affection and responsible emotional expression was way on the back burner of priorities. Societal norms for what has seemed like centuries discouraged it due to layers upon layers of fear of unlocking truths and, heaven forbid, what other people might think. Instead, demands to "stop crying it will be ok", "suck it up", "be strong and work hard or else" were commonplace in parenting across the planet.

As sensitive as I was to the magic around me, I was also extremely affected by the shadow. The forgotten, backlogged and festering energies cried out in sinister ways to get attention. A variety of beings would visit me at night. I would sleepwalk and find myself in different areas of the house where I would wake up, cold and alone.

Filled with fear and rage and not knowing how to truly express myself, I began self-harming at age seven to relieve my frustration. Picking my skin off gave me the chemical adjustment and perceived control over my life, and that, for at least a moment, helped me out of my pent-up rage. I became aware that I chose this life as a warrior, and I was terrified of what my power actually meant. I was afraid of my voice, afraid of my body, I felt awkward and self-aware, and I wanted to hide most of the time. I wanted to be held and share in a safe space what was going on, but I didn't know how. It seemed like no one in my family did. That is why I was here. My path. My purpose. My Legacy.

TO HELP HEAL CYCLES OF EMOTIONAL REPRESSION.

At age five, I started taking dance lessons, and by the time I was eight, I was completely dedicated to being classically trained in ballet. During these years, I was able to connect to my body in a more ethereal way. My stamina was profound and the energy field around me felt so strong. It was an experience of art in motion. Expression through form. This training was such an important foundation for what was to come. It wasn't just training for this particular art form, but an early education on the standards others place upon you if you let them. In ballet, there is a ton of focus on body shape, weight, size, flexibility and muscle tone. If you do not fit the bill, even at an early age, it is made known. There were years where I was nailing it and then years where I fell behind. These fluctuations and the attention to them was intense for a sensitive child like me to process.

Soon enough, puberty hit, and with it came depression. Ballet takes an enormous amount of energy, focus, connection and commitment that was no longer available to me once depression was present, so I made the decision to quit. Some members of my emotionally repressed family circle behaved as if I had signed my own death certificate by quitting. That's a lot of pressure for a teenager. They couldn't hold understanding for others when they didn't have the courage or awareness to hold understanding for themselves. I can see now that they saw my depression and this act of quitting as a spark dying within me. A spark they we proud of. It was hard for them to express their love and their hurt. That was a very painful and complex time for all of us.

My depression deepened. Sometimes I felt like I couldn't move or speak. I would anxiously tell my parents I loved them over and over again, as if wanting more from them. I searched for more support, more affection, and more help from them. They would often respond by being annoyed, frozen or confused, and didn't know how to hold space for me. They did the best they could with what they grew up with. They were both likely scared to process all the sh*t they went through growing up due to generational cycles of tight-holding and avoidance behavior.

As a young teenager, I started to become a bit desperate to ease my mental and emotional state. When the opportunity to smoke weed presented itself at an early age, I was totally on board. What a game changer! I f*cking loved being stoned. I could see color and laugh and have fun! My life turned into a scene out of Dazed and Confused. Promiscuity jumped on board for the ride, followed by alcohol; that seems to go hand in hand with teenage sex. For the first time in this lifetime, I felt what I thought then was fulfillment. I was being touched and loved up, and I was medicating the depression away with booze and drugs. At fifteen years old. This wild ride of ups and downs and hazy shades of ridiculousness continued all throughout my teens.

My twenties were not much different. I continued partying like crazy and being wild. I went to see bands, played in bands, and was rowdy in mosh pits. Seeking approval from others, I contorted my behavior to what I thought cool was. The harder I thrashed, the cooler I was. It was exhausting.

I went to beauty school and started doing hair by the time I was twenty-one. At twenty-two, a dear friend of mine asked if I was interested in partnering on a unique hair gig while he did make-up. Up for anything outside what was typical, I said yes. Little did I know the timeline I was about to step into. It was at a famous strip club! I styled hair for dancers while my bestie at the time did makeup. For dancers. At a strip club. What a rush! It was the underbelly of the entertainment industry and I was behind the scenes. It was like an adult-themed carnival ride the entire fourteen years I was there.

It did not take long to see why I chose this timeline at the club. In the people I connected with during these years, I saw the roots that set the tone. The roots of a common bond: emotional repression, neglect, unhealthy expressions of affection. I saw avoidance behavior like risk-taking and contorting one's behavior to get approval. Those scars run deep: generations deep, DNA deep, subconscious landscape deep and ten bodies deep. Now I understood why I chose this stop along my path. It was another building block to set the foundation as a guide and healer.

In seeing this bond, I let myself start to open up to my own pain a bit. I began to see how things could be if I wasn't proactive about getting help for my own avoidance behaviors. I sought out naturopathic medicine, energy healing and studied laws of the universe. I started to bring these elements to my work at the strip club little by little. I shared my "Oh, f*ck!" moments with the dancers who seemed open to hearing about them. I thought that if I started to make healthier choices, maybe I could inspire even just one other person to do the same. It worked! What an amazing feeling it is to inspire another person even just for a split second. In those moments, I let myself remember the magic I was so connected to as a child. I remembered the Deva realm—the all that is, the light that shines within us all. I began to let it in again and let my light shine.

In my thirties at the strip club, I fell in love. It wasn't my first time falling in love, however this love was a first in many ways. This love was fast like wildfire that continues to burn even today. This love was sparked with a pensive fine artist fresh out of art school. He was sweet and talented, and carried himself around without apology. I was into it. He was actually one of the DJs at the club. I soon learned that he too shared the roots of this common bond of avoidance behavior. His heart was heavy with the tragedy of receiving a family member's sexually abusive behavior. My brain was saying, "Run as fast as you can away from this dude and his adorable damaged goods baggage." But, my instincts said otherwise. So there I was, a couch-surfing strip club hairstylist in love with a hot mess strip club DJ. We almost immediately talked openly of getting married and performing a blood ritual ceremony in the forest to connect our energy for all time. Um, OK, like what? Both of us clung to wanting the gaps in our hearts filled by risky behavior and contorting ourselves to prove something to someone. Little did we know that a month into dating and planning this marriage, a certain blood ritual ceremony had already taken place.

I WAS PREGNANT.

All these years later, I still have that positive pregnancy test sitting on my altar. This was it; this is what the portal of our love was intended for. It was puzzle pieces sliding into place while the angels sing type sh*t. All these building blocks of witnessing and experiencing the effects of emotional repression and unhealthy affection and neglect were setting the foundation for this; to be a mother and a father. We were parents to this star dust vessel of love and truth, the bringer of light, my teacher, my daughter.

During my pregnancy, I found myself a bit frozen when it came to self-awareness and I avoided any real preparations for labor, birth or even actually having a new baby. I was terrified and in a weird space of denial. I often gave attention to the false belief that I could barely take care of myself let alone a child—oh, those sticky layers of healing. Like a baby born in the caul, I was slowing shedding this layer of fear. I mistakenly leaned into wishful thinking without taking actions to support myself or my baby. Well, holy sh*t, did I learn my lesson there. My fear led to a lack of education of my rights and even how my body could work that had me knocking on death's door during her birth.

Then, there she was. After massive third-degree tearing and eyes nearing swollen shut from pushing for over five hours, there she was. I remember being in shock by my beautiful 8.5 pound baby once she was plopped on my belly. We waited to find out her gender, and words can't describe that moment of meeting my baby and finding out that she, was a she.

THAT WAS THE TURNING POINT.

That was the moment I truly committed to healing; the moment our soul contract was signed by all parties. I let go of generations of pain right then and there through what I now know was the channel of joy. Purely and blissfully hysterical. Complete soul connection. Forever, in that moment. Through time and space, my daughter and I met yet again to learn and grow in massive ways.

From that moment, I was committed to the path of healing myself; committed to holding space for others to heal themselves; committed to being a mother; and committed to my Legacy, a Legacy of Love.

I saw in crystal clear detail the effects of emotional repression and neglect that come from withholding healthy expressions of love and physical affection. Now, I was ready to see what was on the other side on the liberated side of expression.

In the first year of my daughter's life and my first year of being a mother, I directed all my love in every possible way to my baby and that love was effortlessly given back to me from her in total and complete alchemy. We were and still are massively connected and massively in love. The freedom that comes with experiencing love like that is completely transformative. Not only was I in love with her, I began to fall in love with myself. I welcomed the Deva realm and exchanged energy with all the magical subtleties of this planet freely and deliberately. I dove headfirst into studying healing arts modalities. During these studies, I experienced the movement of all ten of my bodies while I organically invited generations of tight holding to scream, cry and purge out of me. I did this for years in a safe space with both physical and non-physical guides holding me. Through years of sound and movement, I developed courage around responsibly expressing my emotions in full. With all this energetic focus, I saw the ripple effect of this work. My family lineage started to open and shift in healthier ways. My daughter's daddy confronted his childhood abuser and continues to take healthy action to grow and expand.

THAT'S WHEN I BECAME A PRACTITIONER.

And here we are. Here you are. Here we are together. Yes, you reading this, ready and courageous. I am so proud of you. You see, when I became a mother it wasn't just to my daughter. It was also to myself. I became the embodiment of loving nurture so I could be the warrior and guide for others that I was intended to be in this life. In the words that I say to myself, my daughter and my clients: "You are safe to feel and safe to express. How other people think and feel is not your responsibility. How you think and feel is your responsibility. Where you are is perfect. You are learning and growing with each breath." Liberate yourself and heal the scars that might be contained in your ten bodies through your own sound and movement. You are held, supported and loved.

To be a space holder for others on the journey of finding their own way to love and liberation is the highest honor. For some, it's becoming a parent to another. For others, it's becoming a parent to themselves. With my clients, I ride the dark waves of the layers of trauma and pain that are shed with each sound, each movement, and each emotional release. We ride that wave till we see their Light, their Love, their Legacy.

ABOUT THE AUTHOR

BRANDY KNIGHT

Brandy Knight is the ever-evolving alchemist behind the Healing Arts and Kundalini Yoga practice, Inner Caulling. With a potent blend of different sound and movement modalities, Brandy guides her clients through massive emotional and energetic transformations. Her driving force is to inspire others to purge and transmute any backlogged emotional content that might be blocking the YES vibes available to them. She is a witty West Coast native who is filled with love for her daughter, partner, and kitties.

Website: www.InnerCaulling.com
Instagram: @innercaulling
Facebook: www.facebook.com/brandy.knight.39545
Youtube: www.youtube.com/channel/UCHtFXPDC2YBAJS76-kn372A
Email: innercaulling@gmail.com

8

CAITLIN LYNCH

THE REMEMBERING

It was 2:30 in the morning. I was sitting on the couch in the living room. It was dark, I felt cold. My heart was racing. Tears streaming down my face. I could hear the dog snoring and the gentle hum of the baby monitor.

I was angry, confused, hurt. I felt neglected and suffocated all at once. I found myself in a home, in an environment, in a relationship that I no longer wanted any part of — not one moment longer.

It was a terrible feeling. I quickly resorted to blame. I blamed my husband for everything. I was angry at the way I had been treated for the last five years. I resented the amount of seemingly thankless work I did to maintain the home, take care of our baby, take care of my husband, and manage multiple jobs and degrees. The worst part —I hated myself. I no longer recognized the woman staring back at me in the mirror. Where had Caitlin gone?

Did he do things wrong? Absolutely. But so had I.

As the incredible Elizabeth Gilbert explained similarly in her own words:

"I had actively participated in every moment of the creation of this life. So why didn't I see myself in any of it? The only thing more impossible than staying... was leaving. I didn't want to hurt anybody, I wanted to slip quietly out the back door and not stop running until I reached Greenland."

I read her world famous book, *Eat Pray Love*, and watched the film multiple times before I had even gotten into a relationship with my then husband. I will never forget the moment I finally came to terms with the fact that I no longer wanted to be part of our marriage. When I did, I heard these exact words in my mind. I could feel them resonate deeply in my heart and soul: "I want out."

There was so much shame, so much anxiety, so much animosity, anger, and hatred. Where was my drive, my passion, my love, my excitement? It was gone. I felt as though I had no pulse. I felt as though my very being had been reduced to a ball of anxiety—**my body, neglected and unloved, felt as though it was caging a beautiful spirit that wanted to break free.**

I no longer valued myself. I no longer took care of myself. I had given my power away. My husband, an ambitious and delegating individual, also had his own wounds that he carried. He demanded a lot from me, expecting me to fill roles similar to his parents. His love language was acts of service. We had taken it to a level that could not be sustained.

It took a long time. Eventually I had to come to terms with the fact that I had loved very deeply in our marriage, without loving myself in return.

We both found ourselves in a toxic and seriously co-dependent relationship. How did we come to such a place after six years of marriage? We had overcome many challenges. We moved eight times, including two international moves. We experienced the birth of our son. We bought and sold three properties.

We had just purchased our third home and made a significant amount of money on the sale of our second home. We both had successful careers as NYC teachers. Hadn't we made it past all the trials? Hadn't we proved that we could survive through anything? But that's the thing—we were surviving, not thriving.

How did we get here?

You see, when we met—it was a whirlwind of excitement. We both fell in love. We fell hard and fast. We talked all the time, despite the difference in location. He lived in London and I in New York. After connecting on eHarmony, it was as if we couldn't stay away from each other. Two magnets, completely and totally attracted to each other with incredible infatuation.

That's exactly how it started. Passionate infatuation. Blind love. We rushed into a relationship, without having the difficult conversations first. We knew we wanted each other, and that we were both willing to move for each other. But, we never really discussed much after that.

We never discussed exactly what we each wanted as individuals. We never discussed our individual love languages, our individual passions, and our individual priorities outside of wanting to be with each other. From the start, we both saw the other as able to fill some void we each had within — and that was all that mattered.

We were both young, naive, in love, and unable to understand just how dependent we became on each other—and so quickly. He became the source of my happiness and I the source of his. This was a very dangerous and toxic place to be. Before we knew it, our behavior and priorities became dictated by the other. We both lost ourselves in our relationship.

We have now been divorced for a little over two years and legally separated for longer. Until recently, I've held on to intense anger, animosity, and frustration towards my ex-husband. It was easy for me to blame him for the way I was treated, how controlled I felt, and simultaneously how neglected I felt.

What was much harder was taking responsibility for my contribution to this dynamic. I had told him in a million tiny ways, over and over again, that his behavior was okay.

Should he have known better most of the time? Absolutely.

However, I had also allowed this to go on — he thought nothing was wrong. He thought that everything was wonderful. He thought that his wife loved taking care of everything. I did not. I wanted to be taken care of too.

By the time I began to communicate my wants and needs, I was gaslighted; I was told that I was just stressed or overreacting, my wants and needs going unheard because they seemed foreign, alien. My seemingly "new" wants and needs felt like a threat to him, like I was "changing".

That's when I realized I had to get out. That was the moment I finally understood that what we had been bound by was infatuation and chemistry. It had fizzled out. *What we needed was compatibility and connection—we did not have it.*

We were doomed from the start. If we had taken the time to truly get to know one another, to be honest with ourselves and each other—we would have realized that we were actually not compatible. We have different wants and needs, and too many of our core values do not align.

Despite all of the hurt and the challenges, we both received the greatest gift of our lives from our time together: our son, Jack. He has made us both better human beings, and has inspired the two of us to continue growing, learning, and evolving.

We have also become great teachers to each other. My ex-husband has taught me many things about myself—what I want, what I do not want—and he has taught me many things about life. I know he can say the same about my influence on his life as well.

We had to overcome many challenges with regard to co-parenting our amazing son. We have fought, yelled, cried, and hurt. We have also apologized, listened, and taken the time to understand each other.

Time, space, and introspection has given us the gift of friendship.

I can now say that my ex-husband is no longer my enemy, but a friend. I am happy that he is the father of our son. They care deeply for each other, have fun together, and I know there is a wonderful bond and love between them. I am now able to recognize qualities about him that I appreciate instead of just focusing on the ones I do not align with.

Open, honest, and clear communication got us here. The shift toward facilitating this kind of communication came when I began to vehemently advocate for my wants and needs. When I established clear boundaries, spoke clearly about what I wanted and deserved, and did not settle for anything less, an incredible shift happened. The moment I began valuing and honoring myself was the moment that our relationship began changing for the better.

This is a very powerful, yet extremely painful realization. I could have easily fallen down the spiral of shame by believing all of this was my fault.

Was the whole thing my fault? Was this entire marriage and the conflict that ensued my own manifestation? Absolutely not. We both actively participated in the creation of the life we shared—in the toxic dynamic of codependency.

However, I decided to no longer be part of that dynamic. When that shift happened, the dance could no longer take place. As they say, it takes two to tango.

My therapist gave me incredible advice one day as I was complaining about my ex-husband during the divorce proceedings. I was going on and on about him for the first half of the session. My energy and focus totally on his behavior and the things he was saying. When I finally paused to take a breath, she looked at me calmly and asked:

"Caitlin, what makes you think that your divorce is going to be any different from your marriage?"

This profound question made me realize that divorce alone will not change a relationship. The way we choose to behave and participate in the relationship will change it.

We get to choose how we want to participate in the relationships we have in our lives.

The most important relationship is the one we have with ourselves. It is crucially important that we honor and cultivate our relationship with self. When we do that, we know what we want, we know what we deserve, we can establish healthy boundaries—and we can have healthier and more fulfilling relationships.

No matter where you find yourself in your life, no matter what challenges you have faced with regard to your relationships, we all have that choice.

We can also choose our perspective. We can choose to see life as happening to us as if embracing a victim mentality that will ultimately cage us. Or, we can choose to see life as one of our own making, where each challenge and conflict are an opportunity for growth and learning.

This has become my purpose. As an educator, a mother, a life coach, a writer, and educational reform activist, I am on a mission to help all those who are willing to discover who they were always meant to be; to remember their inner voice and essence.

I have found that Elizabeth Gilbert's concept of the "Physics of the Quest" as outlined in her book *Eat Pray Love* describes this beautifully:

"I've come to believe that there exists in the universe something I call "The Physics of The Quest"—a force of nature governed by laws as real as the laws of gravity or momentum. And the rule of Quest Physics maybe goes like this: 'If you are brave enough to leave behind everything familiar and comforting (which can be anything from your house to your bitter old resentments) and set out on a

truth-seeking journey (either externally or internally), and if you are truly willing to regard everything that happens to you on that journey as a clue, and if you accept everyone you meet along the way as a teacher, and if you are prepared —most of all—to face (and forgive) some very difficult realities about yourself... then truth will not be withheld from you.' Or so I've come to believe."

I am grateful that I now have the ability to say thank you to my ex-husband for being a profound teacher in my life. I am so intensely grateful for the opportunity to rewrite my divorce story.

This incredibly heart-opening and soul-searching experience led me down the path toward remembering myself. You see, life is not about finding yourself. It doesn't really work that way. We haven't gone astray, we aren't an old dollar bill buried in the backseat of the car. Our authentic selves are always with us. She is that beautiful spark inside our hearts while our souls wait patiently for us to remember that she is there, waiting for her flame to be ignited and fed love once again.

Over time, as we are growing up, her flame dwindles. So many of us begin to ignore and hide our authentic selves in childhood. That can continue through adolescence and young adulthood, until the volume of everyone else's noise has become so loud that we can no longer hear our inner voice, our authentic selves, calling out to be loved, to be honored, to be embraced.

Shame, hurt, embarrassment, broken relationships, are all reasons why we hide our authentic selves. When we do this, we become consumed with the expectations and judgments of others.

Maybe your parents or extended family have ideas of who you should become, or your romantic partner has expectations of how you should show up for them, or your friends continually tell you how you should behave to be accepted by others.

The problem with "should-ing" ourselves is that when we focus on what we "should" be doing, or who we "should" be, we are oftentimes listening to outside opinions over everything else. When this happens, we ultimately get lost in the noise of everyone else's voices, while simultaneously drowning out our own.

This may look like accepting the safest career instead of creating a life in the pursuit of our dreams. It could mean that we fall into marriage and parenthood too early, when instead we wanted to travel the world in our youth. It could look like a child who is shunned for being "too loud" or "too silly" or "too bossy" instead of being coached and encouraged to be their authentic selves in a kind and loving way.

Continually "should-ing" ourselves puts us on the road toward settling in response to the perceptions of others instead of listening to our inner voice.

As philosopher Charles Horton Cooley famously said, ***"I am not who you think I am; I am not who I think I am; I am who I think you think I am."***

Let that sink in for a moment.

How many of us are living a perception of a perception of ourselves? Our identities are made up by what our parents, our teachers, our schools, all thought we "should" be. I learned this from my incredible mentor and teacher, Jay Shetty.

When we worry about how others perceive us, we fall into the trap of "should-ing" ourselves. We start saying that we "should" do something or we "should" be someone when we have lost our identity and become overly concerned about what others think of us.

Instead we must listen to our inner voice.

We must take the time each and every day to cultivate a relationship with ourselves. Otherwise, the advice, caring words of concern, straight-up judgments or misunderstandings, and feedback from others will become more than that. Over time, without cultivating our inner-knowing, these voices will become our guides and pull us in all different directions. We may even become dependent on the voices and validation of others; thereby giving our power away to others.

Our inner voice is the one we need to value most. Our relationships with ourselves are the most important relationships we will ever have.

Once we have developed this loving relationship with ourselves, we can expose ourselves to as many experiences, teachers, mentors, and ideas as possible until we can find what our true calling is. That is how we find our purpose.

My pain has become my purpose. For so long, I lived my life based on the perceptions and expectations of others. For so long, I quieted my intuition, my inner voice, my authentic self, to please others and to fit into the narratives that were convenient for society. I ultimately people-pleased my way into depression, anxiety, and fully embraced a life built on low self-worth.

Coming to these realizations was no easy pill to swallow. However, I know I am not alone. I know that many other people have experienced similar situations in their lives and continue to struggle with honoring who they were always meant to be. I fundamentally believe that embracing and loving the self allows us to not only love and embrace each other but help to heal this planet.

The more we are able to love, accept, and forgive ourselves with loving compassion, the more we will be able to extend compassion, love, acceptance, and forgiveness to others; the more we will be able to set healthy boundaries for unwanted behavior; -- the more we will be able to say no when we want to say no and yes when we want to say yes; and the more we will be able to live authentic and wholehearted lives. It starts with us and really begins when we start teaching these skills and facilitating this healing and growth in our children, our adolescents, and our young adults.

It's time we start teaching children to honor and love themselves. It's time we start teaching children how to cultivate their inner voice.

It's time we start unlearning the unproductive and hurtful messages we have adopted about ourselves from other people in childhood through adult life.

It's time we allow each and every single individual to thrive beautifully as they were always meant to.

Let us find it in our hearts to forgive — not just our past partners and others who have hurt us, but ourselves as well.

ABOUT THE AUTHOR

CAITLIN LYNCH

Caitlin Lynch is the founder of Unlearning to Learn - a coaching
service and educational reform platform on a mission to unearth
outdated educational paradigms. Her goal is to rebuild and
restructure our schooling systems with new intentions and fresh
perspectives grounded in ancient wisdom in order to support and
prepare entire school communities to fully embrace lives of purpose,
fulfillment, love, service, and global citizenship. She wholeheartedly
believes that all people are deserving to be who they were always
meant to be, and she is passionate about helping people discover
their dharma, so they may find purpose in this world through
service. Caitlin is a teacher, a mother, a coach, a writer, and a
student. She lives on Long Island, NY with her amazing son, Jack,
and her incredible parents, Patricia and Michael.

Websites: www.unlearning2learn.com
www.caitlin-lynch.medium.com
Instagram: www.instagram.com/iam_caitlinroselynch

9

DANIELLE MASSI, MS, LMFT

FROM REPRESSION TO ASCENSION: THE OVERLAP OF SCIENCE AND SOUL

THE PART WHERE I GOT CANCER

My life changed the week before my 30th birthday, and no one, including me, saw it coming. A seemingly normal, healthy mother of two heads to a routine gynecology appointment and within two weeks is given a diagnosis of cervical cancer. It was like the beginning of a bad Hallmark movie. Cancer? How could this have possibly happened to me? Both my doctors and I were floored, because there were no symptoms, no abnormal previous test results that we could pull from, and no indicators whatsoever that this would be the outcome we would now have to face.

I wrestled with this for quite some time. How could I have possibly developed cervical cancer if I was perfectly healthy?

The short answer is, because I wasn't as healthy as I thought I was.

Health is an overarching term, with a multitude of layers that encompass it. When I believed that I was healthy, it was because I was following the societal rule book for health that I had learned throughout my life. I ate three meals a day, slept eight hours, had a job to go to, and got moderate exercise. I was in a healthy relationship with a loving partner, had a supportive family, and wonderful long-term friendships to rely on. But it turns out, there were things I was actively avoiding—and avoidance and repression are preliminary indicators of disease.

At the time of my diagnosis, I was a licensed psychotherapist with a background in cognitive neuroscience. I had made a career out of understanding that our mental health takes a toll on our physical health, and the mind-body connection is responsible for most (if not all) chronic illnesses that we humans encounter. When my doctors were attempting to find a cause for my cervical cancer diagnosis, they looked only at my body. What they forgot to examine was my mind.

Leading up to my cancer diagnosis, I had experienced significant levels of stress over long periods of time. As a child, my family experienced hardship. My parents did a wonderful job trying to hide this from me, but stress levels are transmittable. What that means is that stress in itself is contagious, especially for those who are highly empathic. I was mercilessly bullied in middle school, raped twice in high school, and went to university at the age of seventeen far from home, in a place where I had no support system. I chose an aggressive course curriculum, majoring in psychology while minoring in cognitive neuroscience, while working two jobs to help ease the burden on my parents. After graduation, I jumped right into a Master's Program where I promptly developed shingles, an illness that is caused by severe stress. After graduation, I opened a private practice that floundered. I quickly got married and had my two children at a time when my business was particularly vulnerable, and I developed postpartum depression after each birth.

Outwardly, my life looked perfect. Inwardly, I was dying inside.

I, like many, had learned to keep moving. That strength comes from picking up your chin, putting a smile on your face, and moving forward. But it turns out that this is a recipe for avoidance, not resilience. When we ignore the impact of the events occurring in our external world, by choosing to repress our emotions and experiences, we are creating a constant state of panic within the body. And this never-ending panic is referred to as chronic stress.

According to various scientific studies, chronic stress has such a significant impact on the immune system that it is the *number one* cause of disease. Chronic stress suppresses the immune system by increasing suppressor T cell and catecholamine, altering acid concentration within the human body, causing plaque buildup in the arteries, and altering the production and reception of certain neurotransmitters in the brain. Ultimately, our stress level is slowly killing us from the inside out.

And in a society where appearance is everything, repressing our emotions has become the standard. We are doing everything wrong when it comes to our health. And unlearning repression begins with the acknowledgement that we are making ourselves sick.

EXCAVATING THE SHADOW

We can unlearn repression fairly easily by daring to examine what Carl Jung coined "The shadow". The shadow is just a term for the unconscious mind, which is essentially everything lying beneath the surface of our awareness that we repress, either on purpose or unintentionally. The unconscious mind is an innate feature of the brain, and is a sort of landing area for trauma.

Let me explain how this process happens: imagine the brain as a type of sorting system. Every piece of input that the brain receives needs to be categorized and sorted so that the brain knows how to process it. When the brain needs access with a certain input, it goes to the conscious mind, where you remain fully aware of its presence. For an input the brain is so familiar with that it no longer needs to actively interact, it goes to the subconscious mind; this is like being on autopilot. And for the input that the brain doesn't want you to interact with because it is potentially harmful or traumatic, it goes to the unconscious mind, where it can be thoroughly repressed.

Every hardship you have faced, every trauma you have incurred, and every extreme negative emotion that you have felt, lives within the shadow. You can imagine how dense the shadow becomes as we continue to repress for years at a time. The weight of what lies within the shadow is an enormous burden for our soul to carry.

And that was invariably true for me. While I wasn't consciously aware of what was weighing me down, I was undoubtedly carrying the weight of my accumulating shadow over the course of my thirty years of life. And as long as I continued to repress my shadow, I kept myself in a state of chronic stress.

Now, from this new vantage point, my cervical cancer seems like it was inevitable. If I were to force myself into a state of chronic stress, disease was unavoidable. And that, my friends, is where my mission in life comes in.

I want you (yes, you!) to live an incredible, abundant, beautiful, healthy life. I want you to have little to no shadow to contend with, because you actively choose to examine the experiences you might otherwise repress, and create new paradigms within your life. I want you to choose yourself every time—because you are worthy of living a life of ease.

HACKING THE MIND-BODY CONNECTION

You have the power to heal yourself from any long-term, chronic ailment that you may face. Let that sink in. No medications or surgeries required; it's the power that already lies within your body, mind, and soul. It may seem too good to be true, but in fact it's been proven by research time and time again that human beings are extremely resilient and capable of creating change with only the power of their minds.

It all starts with a choice: the choice to create an internal and external environment that promotes health and wellness at all times, with no exceptions.

Our entire world is shaped through a specific mind-body loop. It begins with our experiences; everything that we experience through sensory means is taken in by the mind. The mind processes these experiences by producing a chemical reaction (also known as an emotion) which is used to communicate with the body. These chemicals send the message to our body about how we should physically respond, and our body acts accordingly by sending blood and oxygen wherever it needs to go. Then, the body completes the loop by sending a message back to the mind in the form of a thought, sometimes referred to as an ego message, to make sense of the loop and what it means for the person who just had the experience.

This entire mind-body loop wires the brain, and the more consistent the loop is, the more hardwired we become. This loop constantly repeats, causing us to have lives that follow a specific trajectory. Once our brain is hardwired, we subconsciously seek to recreate the same loop infinitely because it requires less effort for the mind and body to process it. This is exactly why we have such a hard time creating change, and why we have such an easy time creating discomfort and disease in our lives.

Until now.

Imagine you were to make a choice to examine those things that have become hardwired within your brain. What if you were to trace them back to their origin and think about the emotions that are tied to them, how it physically feels within your body, and what it makes you think? What you might find is that these hardwired items are a series of choices that your mind has made for you about who you are and what your life should be.

Now imagine a scenario where you choose to interrupt this feedback loop by actively overriding all of these data points?

Let's use an example from my own rewiring process. When I began to examine my feedback loops, I noticed that I had a hardwired pathway of needing control in my life. I had many experiences where I felt out of control: being poor, being bullied, being raped, developing cancer, and so on. The emotions tied to feeling out of control for me were fear, shame, and anger. Physically within my body, that would drive me into a state called Fight or Flight, where adrenaline and cortisol would be produced and blood and oxygen would move into the places in my body that would assist me in running away, fighting back, or freezing like a deer in headlights. And the thought most associated with being out of control was that I was unable to protect myself.

Hacking the mind-body connection requires us to rewrite the narrative, and that is exactly what I had to do. The victim mentality that I had learned had kept me in a permanent state of chronic stress, so I needed to create a new story. And so, I decided to rewrite the narrative as a hero's journey instead of a victim's.

When I examine my experiences with fresh eyes, I notice that I was someone who faced insurmountable odds and survived. When I look at these experiences, I think of myself as someone who overcame tragedy and created beauty from it. And when I see the experience in this way, I allow myself to feel the emotions of gratitude, acceptance, and even joy. These emotions have the opposite effect on my physical body, causing the blood and oxygen to flow to the areas that need healing. And then I come full circle back to the thought that I'm the hero of my story, and that my life has been beautiful.

All it takes is a choice. You can actively choose to release the version of you reading this book today, and choose to create a legacy of your own by taking your power back and becoming the author of your own story.

LIVING OUT MY LEGACY

Two years post cervical cancer, I am the healthiest I've ever been. I no longer feel stress in my life, even when I'm overcoming something hard, because I know how to help my mind process the event consciously to prevent it from falling into the shadow.

I now own a holistic healing center in Philadelphia, PA where I employ eight wellness professionals of different backgrounds who help people tap into their limitless ability to heal from the inside out.

I'm the co-host of a spirituality podcast, where we bring holistic healers from around the world onto the show to share their medicine. They talk about their dark night of the soul, and how they have used their innate abilities to fully heal from the shadow that they once carried. These guest experts are a perfect example of our potential to heal, no matter the circumstances.

I co-host a self-care conference in the city of Philadelphia called SELF(ISH)philly, where we bring in the best healing resources and experts from the area to show women that there are so many pathways to health and wellness. We teach them to break free of the outdated paradigm of merely reducing the warning signs of illness, and instead help them work from a place of prevention to ensure their long-term health and happiness.

And I myself have become a master shadow worker, helping release women from the unconscious traumas they cannot discover on their own to help them find their way to healing they never thought possible. I've worked with thousands of students, and that number grows by the day. And my hope is that that number continues to grow until every person on this planet recognizes their own innate ability to overcome their biology and heal from the inside out.

My legacy is the health and wellness of a generation of people who are sick of being sick. Of the ones who are ready to overcome the odds, and learn how to surpass what they thought was physically possible for human beings to accomplish. To rid themselves of the societal norms about what we are supposed to do, and to embrace the path that they themselves choose to lay out before their own feet. My legacy is to use all of the hardships I have faced to teach you that you do not need to wait for rock bottom to change your life. You can create change from a place of ease, grace, and love just as easily. My legacy is to help you create yours.

ABOUT THE AUTHOR

DANIELLE MASSI, MS, LMFT

Danielle Massi, M.S., LMFT, is a licensed psychotherapist and master shadow worker and the owner of The Wellness Collective, a holistic healing center in Philadelphia, PA. With her background in psychology, cognitive neuroscience, and shadow work, Danielle is able to help women unlock the mind and use it as a tool to rewire the physical body. She believes that stress is the root cause of most ailments and diseases, and has made it her mission to educate the masses and give them the tools to take their healing into their own hands.

Through her virtual coaching programs, Danielle teaches people how to hack the mind and body by using the unconscious shadow as a tool for massive growth and abundance. Danielle is the co-host of the Embrace Your Light podcast and the co-founder of the SELF(ISH)philly conference, an annual self-care conference for women in Philadelphia, PA.

Website: www.iamdaniellemassi.com

www.wellnessphl.com
Instagram: www.instagram.com/iamdaniellemassi
www.instagram.com/wellnessphl
Facebook Group: https://www.facebook.com/groups/ClarityClubDM
Email: Dmassi@wellnessphl.com

GINA FRANCES

WOMB AWAKENING: A COMING HOME

To the people who bleed out of their vaginas:
We all bleed the same color.
We drip sweet nectar from in between our thighs,
no matter the color of our eyes
or the colors of those who merged together, in Divine assemble
to create our physical temple,
No matter the color of the skin that we are blessed to resemble,
black white brown orange pink purple blue...
If sisters desire to shift the narrative, there is so much more we must do.
Oh woman, recognize the power between your thighs,
the ancient vessel of creation within you is so wise
You hold the keys to the answers, the waters within you are flowing
It's not your fault they've stripped you from that innate knowing
If they bled every month, and did not die,
they would not tell us that we lie.

For most of my life, I forgot. You, sister, may have forgotten, too.

I forgot who I was; a veil of illusion painted over my eyes, as if I was living and seeing through a lens fogged by manipulation, suppression, limitations, and rules that were not my own. This clouded and dirty lens I was living life through told me that I was not enough; that I was not good enough, thin enough, smart enough, or pretty enough. It also told me that I was too much; I was too moody, too bossy, too bitchy, too loud, too obnoxious, too pretty, too thin.

I was not only seeing and living life through a distorted lens, I was also hearing this distortion as well. I began looking down at a body I had once loved and adored for her strength and stamina, to instead see a body towards which I could offer nothing but hateful words and criticism. There were voices inside my head as well that I simply could not shake. They would shout at me daily until it was all I could hear. Constant demeaning, criticizing, and punishing words that I had never heard before. These voices also taught me that my worth was based on how much I was 'doing' and how 'good' I was at it. They told me to seek validation outside of myself; to place my power in the hands of others—especially men.

It all unfolded when I started taking those pills.

What you are about to read is the story of a remembering. I encourage you to hold awareness around your breath as you read, stopping now and then to place a hand or two on your heart and womb. Please note that I use the term womb throughout this chapter to refer to the energetic wombspace as a whole, whether you have a physical womb or not.

The first time I got my period, I hid it from my mother and friends. I didn't tell anyone; a wave of embarrassment and shame washed over me as I sat on the toilet, confused and scared with not a clue what to do. I wasn't taught anything about my period or menstrual cycle, aside from the dry education we received in health class that barely told girls what was happening in their bodies, yet told us to deal with it, get some pads or tampons and avoid getting pregnant. So yeah, with that clinical surface level education, plus the disconnect from the wisdom of the womb within recent generations of my maternal lineage, why would I think of my cycle as sacred, magic, and holy?

Like many young girls, I was soon given hormonal birth control pills as the fix for my monthly 'problems'. "Here, take these magical pills! They will fix you; and by that we mean simply mask the underlying issues and disconnect you from your power source as a woman and intuition! No worries, it's totally safe!"

I spent about eight years of my teen and young adult life unknowingly manipulated by artificial hormones that completely altered me inside and out. This birth control was that veil of illusion.

Fast forward to 2017 when I chose to follow my heart from Australia to the sacred fertile land of Mother Bali. In the same month that my time in Australia was expiring, so too was my birth control. In order to get more, I needed to visit my doctor back in America—but I was on the other side of the world. So back then what I thought of as a minor transition is now what I see as one of the greatest gifts God has given me, and in turn, the legacy that I am here to leave behind.

Deciding to come off of hormonal birth control, though the portal it would open was unintentional and unbeknownst to me, was the most divine synchronicity life has ever presented me with. It was the moment one chapter closed, the veil of illusion lifted, and another chapter began. More so, a new book began. I now refer to this moment as the conception of my legacy.

It was as if the veil was being peeled away. Every passing day, week, and month I shed yet another layer. I was like a snake perpetually outgrowing her own skin, feeling more raw and exposed, yet ultimately more liberated with each layer. Each time I showed up for myself or shared my story with someone and exposed the truth of my journey of eating disorders, anxiety, and pain, another layer fell away.

Months went by without flooding my body with a cocktail of manipulative hormones, and I was coming closer and closer home to myself. It was confusing, confronting, exciting, and also quite terrifying. My ego, my identity, and who I thought I was were all dying in order to be reborn. I would cycle through days, weeks, even a couple of months of depression, deep sadness, and confusion. My body was changing, I was changing, and I had no guidance. I was terrified of truly letting others in, and my heart closed off in a way only I could know. I didn't understand what was happening. Yet there was a deep knowing inside of me that this was the journey I was meant to be on.

As time went on and my natural period did not return, I actually thought it was pretty awesome that I wasn't having to worry about having a period. Without cycling, I was able to fit myself better into the patriarchal model of living, and isn't that what we're all meant to do? No horrible premenstrual cramps, no acne, no need to buy tampons...life was great without a period!

While in a session with my massage therapist about six months later, she was working on my feet and discovered some incredibly tender and painful spots. I remember squirming in discomfort as I heard her say, "Is there anything going on with your reproductive system?" I lay there, reflecting on the past six months without a period, thinking, "Well...there's actually *nothing* going on down there." She gently encouraged me to stop ignoring the signs my body was giving me and to listen; to seek support, and give this attention.

At that point, I was severely burnt out. As a corporate health and fitness professional, I was teaching more than six fitness classes a week, offering personal training, and on top of that, starting my own health and wellness coaching business on the side. I was exhausted, fatigued, underweight, and undernourished. Not only was my physical body undernourished, my soul was undernourished. My creative expression was unfed, my feminine life force was dormant; my womb was vacant. Cobwebs. No lights. No life. No pleasure. No play. No devotion. Yet, I had no idea, because I had not yet experienced an awakened womb. I had not yet remembered.

Soon after the event with my massage therapist, the synchronicities began to weave. I could feel Her, the divine Mother, Shakti, speaking through sensations in my body. She was speaking to me through the people I was meeting, opportunities that were presented to me, and events that were unfolding. I quickly became enthralled with this path of feminine remembering and womb healing. I began dancing. I began speaking to my womb. I began attending women's circles and incorporating ritual, devotion, and sensuality into my day to day routines.

I began to remember.

My womb guided me to slow down, to take more breaks, to have fun. She guided me to change my diet, to stop constantly fasting and eating raw. When I met her with resistance, She nudged at me lovingly, like a gentle, deeply wise woman within me, guiding the way. My ego had to take a seat and allow my womb to guide the way. I chose to shift my eating habits to eat for my womb, while my mind was still stuck in disordered eating behaviors. I chose to eat more regular meals and more grounding foods. I chose to substitute yin for HIIT, long walks in nature for cardio pump, to nourish my womb. This was not an easeful transition; the aversion I met was so strong. Old patterns and old stories of who I was were so deeply ingrained, like deep rivers carved through my mind and body. Choosing to carve out new pathways was edgy, scary, and challenging, yet it felt like I was being taken and guided by a force out of my control. It was like a golden pathway was being unfolded before my eyes, and with every step I took, the walkway appeared.

After a couple of months since altering my lifestyle, I chose to give the medical system one more shot. The doctor did a series of tests and scans, reporting that I was one of the healthiest people she had seen in a while. She was confused and at a loss for why my period had not returned. At that moment, I felt and heard my womb speak to me. This was something that the medical system would not be able to help with. This stemmed from a deep disconnect to my body as a woman and a loathing towards being in a female body that I had not yet allowed to surface. I was carrying the wounds of the women in my lineage who did not appreciate their female bodies, who were convinced and told by society that they were only here to reproduce and give pleasure away to others. The women who came before me who were told that being a woman is difficult.

I was carrying the pain of the women who had forgotten the wisdom of their wombs.

In October of 2017, my body screamed at me to take a break. I even sprained my left ankle, which I came to learn was the feminine side of the body. "Okay, okay, God, Universe, Divine...I HEAR YOU! I'll take a break. I'll finally listen," were my stubborn thoughts as I surrendered to the wisdom of my body.

I'll never forget the drive down to Uluwatu, Bali that day. The sun was shining down on me, and I felt an immediate shift in energy when I got closer to the coast. I felt space around me and space within me. Something in my womb shifted and my breath softened and relaxed. I felt tingles within my womb, like a candle flame was flickering on; I felt the dance of soft light hit and a gentle breeze touch the corners where the cobwebs once were. That evening on the beach, I could feel my womb's calling becoming louder. I could feel her trying to speak to me. Something was changing. My cells were rearranging.

I got up to go for a walk down the beach. One after another, these beautiful cowrie shells appeared under my toes. This shell is known as a symbol of fertility and the feminine in many cultures— something that a wise elder shared with me once. One by one, as the shells guided me down the beach, I felt tears welling up in the corners of my eyes. With each shell that I picked up, I could feel my womb pulsate. I felt Mother Earth beneath my feet, below me, and yet simultaneously within me. As I made my way onto the rocks, the sound of the waves drowned out anything that wasn't the present moment and tears began streaming down my face. I wept and wept, as if I was shedding all of the tears I had not allowed myself to shed. As if I was shedding not only my tears, but the tears of my ancestors. These were the unshed tears of those who came before me. As I stood on the rocks, I knew that I was not alone. I felt the presence of other women around me, holding me, crying with me, standing tall with me. My womb was awakening and the barren space that was once there was coming alive. I felt my bleed arriving.

When I got back to my room that evening, my *yoni* released the first drops of blood I had seen in over a year. They were the first drops of true menstrual blood that I had seen in nearly a decade. The emotions that washed over me remain unexplainable; it was euphoric and out of body—it was a coming home.

As my womb danced and the blood flowed, I felt a wave of remembering flood over me, through me, and around me. I was drenched in this red and gold remembering.

In that moment, I knew.

I knew that this is what I was here to do; that this is my work in this world. As my body released and let go that week, I also let go of any remnants of who I once was: the wounded little girl, the misguided little girl, the confused little girl, and all the parts of me that were fed by patriarchal conditioning and fear-based narratives. Every cycle since then has been a release and creation of space for *me and all of me:* my raw, wild power as a woman. I realized that my menstrual cycle was not something to be shamed or tamed, ridiculed or hidden. That it was medicine, it was magick. I remembered that our sacred blood is the most potent medicine that female-bodied people are gifted with. I remembered the power of not only my womb, but the wombs of people all over the world.

Since this awakening, I've been supporting hundreds of women like you, all over the world, in remembering the power and wisdom that exists within their womb and menstrual cycle. I have assisted women in bringing periods back after months or years of not having a cycle. I have supported women coming off hormonal birth control and IUDs to reclaim their cycle as sacred. I support leaders stepping into their power and claiming their sovereignty and potency as female-bodied people. I teach women how to work with the wisdom that their cycle is their *super power*.

You may have been taught, whether directly or indirectly, that your cycle is a nuisance that gets in the way of your success. Darling, I am here to scream from the rooftops that it is your key to success!

When you deny and reject one part of you, you are denying and rejecting all of you. You were put on this planet with a womb and a period for a reason; instead of using up all of your energy to fight against it, what if you surrendered to the flow of it? What if you allowed yourself to get washed away in the chaos of what it means to be a woman and become enchanted by it? What if you allowed the very thing that allowed you to be birthed into this world to become your legacy; to become your superpower?

My womb is my legacy. It is the legacy God gifted me with because my womb's imprint extends beyond just me; it has impact on the lives of those who are yet to come and those who have come before. When one womb wakes up, the one beside it does, too. When we heal and remember, Mother Earth heals, too.

The legacy of my womb will continue to light up and awaken the wombs of generations and generations to come. I am here to remind you that your wisdom exists within, my love. Look down. Place your hands over your wombspace. This wellspring of life, this portal of potential, She holds everything you will ever need. **She holds your legacy.**

Your pelvis is the wellspring for all of creation—the birthplace of life itself.
Your yoni is a portal to divinity, your labia the gatekeepers to the temple.
the raw wild nature of She
exists within you and me
When will you see it that way?
Take back your power & honor your boundaries. Commit to yourself first, devote to yourself. Make love to yourself as you desire to be made love to by another.
When you are connected to the power & + erotic energy in your pu$$y portal,

you are connected to it everywhere. Your super power & gifts are awakened, like a
bear from its long hibernation.
Place your hands on your wombspace,
Close your eyes & breathe,
Feel the rise & fall,
Feel yourself breathe life back in,
Ask this space what it needs and deserves.
Does it have any messages?
Ask, just ask. Give it a go and listen. Wait. Be patient.
Your womb & yoni must feel safe
& feel trust to open to you or anyone else.
Build a relationship with this sacred space & watch how life shifts & dances
before your eyes.

I love you,
xx
Gina

ABOUT THE AUTHOR

GINA FRANCES

Gina Frances is an Embodiment Guide and Womb Based Business Coach. She guides female-bodied leaders to form a sacred connection with their womb space, honor their inner seasons with cyclical wisdom, sync their business with their menstrual cycle, and lead in life with pleasure. After 8 years on hormonal birth control and a 13 month journey of bringing her cycle back naturally, she was awakened to her mission in this world. Through 1:1 coaching, transformational group courses, workshops, and retreats, Gina bridges science and sacred. She educates leaders about their body and its rhythmic cycles, while creating more confidence, flow, and connection in their lives and career. Gina is the visionary's doula; she holds accountability to her clients' mission with divine feminine vision. Gina is originally from New Jersey and now lives her dream life in Australia where she is studying Herbalism and pursuing a Master's Degree in Sexology.

Website: www.ginafrances.com

Instagram: www.instagram.com/iamginafrances
Facebook: www.facebook.com/iamginafrances5

11

HAILEY PARKES

WE ARE THE LIGHT ONES, WE CAME HERE TO WAKE UP HUMANITY.

The Remembering.
The Awakening.

To the beautiful soul reading this chapter,

I see you.
I feel you.

I am you and you are me.
We are connected in more ways than one.
In unity, in love, in wholeness.

Before you read this chapter, I ask that you have an open mind, a loving heart, and compassion for yourself & you honour where you're at on your journey right now.

As you fully immerse yourself into these pages I ask that you *trust* that you were divinely guided here by your angels, guides, ancestors, beings of light, and loved ones born and past.

I ask that you listen to the whispers from your soul as you read this, and notice the inspiration you feel at how amazing life can be.

Writing these words filled me with absolute passion and excitement, knowing that it was going to land in your lap one day.

Because the word *"legacy"* speaks so true to my heart and spirit. It's ingrained in my DNA, every cell of my body. In all of my past lives and this one too.

A word that has been calling me since my first cry on my mother's chest. A word that called me so deeply into the work I'm doing today as an adult.

It's the first word that comes to mind when I think of *why I'm here.*

It means putting a stamp on the future and making a contribution to the world.

To create such an impact that even generations after we leave this earthly plane,

We can be remembered for the grace, love and light we gifted to others through our presence and leadership.

So, as I begin to write these words, I want you to know that my definition of legacy may be different from yours and there is no "right" or "wrong"; it's simply our own perception & belief system. The same goes for our definition of *"purpose".*

For me, *purpose* isn't some final destination we arrive at.

It's not something we just wake up to one day.
It's a lifelong journey of healing, learning, and growing.

Accepting, acknowledging, and applying.

> *"So, when I combine the words LEGACY + PURPOSE...*
>
> *I see it as the perfect math equation for our lives.*

"It's a little hard at times, it challenges you, but it's always worth the focus and it always gets summed up."

LEGACY + PURPOSE = LIFE

- Hailey Parkes

There was a time when I almost gave up on myself.

But I didn't.

Instead, I dug to the deepest depths of my soul to stretch myself a little more.

Even though I had a whole spirit team cheering me on and guiding me home to remember why I came here, it was still one of the most difficult things I've ever had to push past.

I still had to come to terms with the fact that all of my *pain* in my physical body was simply negative emotions trapped inside me.

Then the penny dropped.

"The more work I do on myself, the more I heal...the more I can give back to the world and the more conscious I become...therefore, living out my mission & serving my contract."

It was that realisation, that gave me the courage & support I needed to continue doing the inner work. I started to gain clarity on my purpose, and once I got familiar with this process, I was always guided.

So here I am, sitting by the ocean, pouring my heart out into a book that I know is going to inspire many around the world to connect with their intuition and use their guides. But then, a loud voice drops in, and an overwhelming feeling of love surrounds my auric field.

.   .   .

Another one of my guides comes through with the following message;

"Hello star seed, I am one of your guides, a being from a group called the "Pleiadians".
You and I are the same. We incarnated from a star called Pleiades.

Your soul did not originate from this earth like most humans, but you already know this.

Your physical body, the vessel your soul is held by on this planet, was created to bring your spirit back to Earth in this lifetime to carry out a BIG mission.

You have experienced life in other corners of the galaxy and we have met many times before. Unfortunately, your level of consciousness cannot yet remember this.

I am one of your Pleiadian guides, and you have many others like me that you will interact with and learn from very soon.

We are all beings of light. Our civilization evolved millions of years ago and our DNA has been used to breed many humans.

It's important that you understand you have a big mission to carry out here. If you follow our guidance, your health & finances will be looked after. So please don't worry anymore.

For you must focus only on this mission, and if you are successful, you will be rewarded in more ways your human mind cannot comprehend.

So, child, I am here to help you along the way. You can call on me when you need clarity, love, and support.

I am always with you. In your astral travels at night, we are together more than you can remember by the morning.

We have taken you on our ship many times before. Your human mind remembers a recent time, and for that, we are very fortunate.

We want you to know that there will be times where you will feel like giving up, like taking off with us and never coming back. We know you feel alone and misunderstood here on earth, but that's okay.

We are with you in these moments and we want you to find comfort in knowing this. We are even with you right now while you wipe the tears off your face.

You see, star seed, Human life on this planet isn't supposed to be easy for you. You didn't originate from here.

It's part of your soul evolution.

So when you find yourself in these dark places, alone and confused,
we want you to call on us to seek unconditional love & light.

When you ask, you will receive.

So you see, my guides help me a lot in life.. but mainly for this mission to be carried out.

To go into the darkness and face the shadow, to do the inner work, to accept all parts of myself and integrate all the learnings. The work never ends. It's lifelong.

As I healed parts of my childhood trauma, my ancestral wounds and lineage, I started becoming more *conscious.*

I became conscious of where I was at, and where I was going. *I found myself.*

I found who I was at the core, beyond the physical appearance, the online presence and the conditioning of my childhood programming.

I started to WAKE UP.

The Work.

The Inner guidance.

I woke up to the illusion, I came out of the matrix and remembered why I'm here.

My mission in this lifetime.

The contract I signed before I incarnated.

My place in the world. I started to use my gifts more.

I started to speak to my guides. I asked them for many things and I still do—I always will.

I asked for clarity, guidance, love, support, encouragement and certainty.

I asked them for signs that I'm on the right path. I asked them if I accepted this mission before I came here, would I be rewarded for the work I am doing now and will I be rewarded by changing more lives than I am now?

They answered in many moments, "YES."

through whispers, sounds, signs, downloads, messages, synchronicities.

All of it.

So I went to work on myself, more and more.

I connected with them every moment of every day.

Through my thoughts, speaking to them while driving in the car, in meditation, in stillness.

In astral travels, in writing, channelling, and in connecting to nature.

Staying grounded and trusting in the infinite possibilities that they held for me was key to this work. But most importantly, honouring myself through self-love practices and looking after my health were all crucial parts of this connection with them and the divine.

I anchored in love more. I didn't worry about toxic people or negative vampire suckers.

I had many encounters with people of what I refer to as *"reptilian"* which is a type of soul that originates from another constellation. They come in human form, but their soul is of reptilian descent.

Most of them are beings that are toxic, negative, ego-driven, and always seeking to create destruction and divide wherever they go.

The reptilian beings intervened on planet earth and began interbreeding with humans thousands of years ago. Not physically; however they did do this with manipulation of human coding and DNA.

Not all souls in "reptilian" human form originate from their constellation. Some are hijacked by these dark beings & possessed by a reptile from outer space.

They can be seen in high places in world governments and places like that. Everyone should do their own inner work to gain clarity, and look a little closely at the current dynamics and agendas playing out in world.

I've accepted that not all souls are anchored in the light, and that's okay. I have developed compassion and empathy and I pray for them every day.

As I started to awaken and open up to my gifts, I was able to better trust the guidance & the divine plan. The *kundalini* energy within me was rising, and I felt it charge through my body in waves that were almost uncontrollable at times.

I had to seek help in all areas. I manifested human guides so I could really start to step into my power and be the light leader I was born to be.

I knew that at this point, if I manifested all the people I needed to get this mission off the ground, it could reach others so much faster!

It started with becoming an NLP practitioner, coach & certified timeline therapist in March 2020. I experienced such a huge transformation as a client doing timeline therapy, which is a healing modality I did over the phone for six weeks prior to discovering the NLP course.

For those that don't know what NLP & Timeline Therapy is, let's pause here.

NLP stands for "Neuro-linguistic Programming", which means;

Neuro: *"the mind" through which our experience is processed via the five senses: visual, auditory, kinaesthetic, olfactory, gustatory.*

Linguistic: *"the language" and other non-verbal communication systems through which our neural representations are coded, ordered and given meaning. Ranges from pictures, sounds, feelings, tastes, smells to words including self-talk.*

Programming: *"our communication" and the ability to discover and utilize the programs that we run in our neurological systems to achieve our specific and desired outcomes; our communication to ourselves and others.*

In other words, NLP is how to use the language of the mind to consistently achieve our specific and desired outcomes in life.

I had been working in real estate and had been training sales agents and doing office management for over seven and a half years. I loved it, but I knew there was so much more out there for me.

So when I became qualified, I took a giant leap of faith, trusted myself and my guides, and quit my 9-5 to start my business.

Within just two weeks of starting my business, I made more money as a coach than I did in six weeks of working as an office manager in my job.

I knew this was just the start of my purpose-driven work, and merely an opening and stepping stone to this path I'm on now.

I hit the ground running. I went all in. I called on my guides for help to seek out the people I needed to get it started.

Not just in business but in health and relationships too.

I quickly learned I was a "manifesting generator" in human design, which explains a lot about my effortless manifestations.

I found people for everything I needed, and fast. From business coaches to health practitioners to therapists and even friends, I had so many people move into my circle, it felt like magic.

It quickly appeared to be a gift I never knew I had. So I went with it.

I used this gift to source the right people, materials, information & systems to get this mission started. I started tapping into my gifts as a Psychic Medium, Channeler, Coach & Healer to create the foundations needed to begin.

I went deeper into my healing journey and stayed grounded as much as possible.

I had such a crystal clear vision and I knew I was *unstoppable.*

I was very in my masculine a lot of the time because, during my childhood trauma, I was so heavily anchored in this energy of survival.

I lived a very traumatic childhood, with my mum being a heroin user and my dad caught up in crime. I never felt safe. Unfortunately, my dad passed away in prison and was tragically murdered when I was twelve, so the masculine was nowhere to be found in my early years as a young teenager.

I felt I had no choice but to step into Dad's role of being protection for my siblings and my mum's leaning post.

But now, being so heavily in my masculine has had an impact on my health later in life. It led to a diagnosis of an autoimmune condition called "Fibromyalgia" just two and a half years ago.

I've been healing this condition holistically every day since. But it's not something I can heal overnight; I'm still working on it today with some fantastic holistic therapists who I know, like, and trust. My guides help me with this too.

The Legacy to come.

As my journey unfolds and I continue to type these words, it leads me to think about these past twelve months. And I think it's probably time I start talking about my partner now, don't you think? (Ha-ha) For he is part of this mission, and the other half to my soul evolution.

Thomas Meyer, the love of my life.

The man that believes in me and loves all parts of me unconditionally.

The man that healed my broken heart thirteen years after my dad's passing.

The man that helped me feel safe in my feminine for the first time as an adult.

He's the yin to my yang energy and the calm to my storm. He grounds me, protects me, and makes me feel held.

We are not perfect. No one is. But what I love most is the magic we share in times of vulnerability.

We are so proud of the relationship we have today and dedicated to learning from each other to grow and become the best versions of ourselves, so we can complete this mission together.

Though a short relationship, we have done more healing and growing in a few years together than some do in their entire life.

The day I met Tom, it was game over for me.

We met in the middle of Belgium at the Tomorrowland festival on the other side of the world while both on our European summer travels.

We danced our way into the early hours of the morning and talked each other's ear off in a hotel room. We ate pasta and watched Vampire Diaries. That was his choice; never seen the show in my life!

He was a complete gentleman. So kind, caring, all around respectful. I saw many parts of my Dad inside him, and that's what felt like home to me. So humble and so warm.

We had deep and meaningful conversations that blew each other's mind. The synchronicities, especially in numbers, were not coincidence, nor was the timing of our childhood trauma and the events that had taken place in both our lives leading up to that night.

We discovered that we basically lived the same childhood, in parallel to each other.

We fell for each other quickly, and before I knew it, I finished my solo travels eight weeks later and came back to Melbourne, moved into his place a few months later, and the rest is history. We've been madly in love ever since.

We've always known everything was divinely planned, and the universe was always guiding us.

We trusted our internal compass and found healing, peace, love and joy in all areas of life together, as a team.

We know we met for a higher purpose and it sends shivers down my spine writing these words because I have such a deep knowing that the journey ahead is one that Change the lives of many.

You see, we're not here to just "exist".

We're not here to work, have babies, retire & pass over…

No, no.
Not us.

We are the light ones.

We came here to wake up humanity"

-Hailey Parkes

ABOUT THE AUTHOR

HAILEY PARKES

Hailey Parkes is a Speaker, Psychic Medium, Certified Timeline Therapist & Spiritual Teacher. She is the host of "The Light Ones" Podcast & a leading voice for the next generation, empowering them to heal, awaken and transform their life. With huge life experience and a traumatic upbringing, Hailey's story is one that will inspire many around the world. Hailey's mission is to help raise the collective consciousness through speaking, mediumship, teaching & facilitating. She passionately guides individuals who are ready to serve at the highest level to create massive impact. Hailey facilitates soul circles, workshops and retreats around Australia and is ready for global expansion.

Podcast: The Light Ones: https://podcasts.apple.com/au/podcast/the-light-ones/id1554819070
Website: www.haileyparkes.com
Instagram: www.instagram.com/hailey.parkes/
Facebook: www.facebook.com/Haileyparkescoaching

12

HEATHER ROBINSON

EMBODYING THE MOTHER ARCHETYPE

Motherhood changed my life. Not just because it has stolen a lot of sleep and I do way more laundry, or because I have this amazing bundle of love to brighten my days. No, it changed my life because it made me show the f*ck up. Not just for my son, but for myself. It made me consider the legacy I'll leave behind and make profound changes in my life by integrating and embodying the deep healing and many lessons that came along with it.

For many years, I invested a lot of time and energy into self-development. I'm always alchemizing my experiences and growing into a more aligned version of myself. I'm a Scorpio after all, forever transforming. Entrepreneurship reinforces this journey and requires I show up fully for both the self and the business. It's a lot like motherhood in that way. For a long time, I did "all the things": I took care of myself, did healing work, practiced my craft, and worked on my business. I was convinced I was doing everything I could, or should, to be successful, and that one day I'd wake up and my work will have paid off and I could say, "I made it!"

In 2018, I had a successful business and a budding career as a newborn photographer and doula, but after five years I still felt lost and unfulfilled. I felt my soul calling to find alignment and began transforming my business, unsure of where it was headed. I signed up for a coaching program, hired a business coach, and then enrolled in another program. They surely had the answers I was seeking! I then proceeded to resist some of the basic things my coach suggested I do. I didn't realize how much at the time, and I had no idea how much it was holding me back.

After revamping my business, I felt like I had finally reached that point of waking up a "success"! But then, it all fell apart. Following a traumatic experience, I found myself moving across the country to follow my joy, or run from the trauma, and start fresh. I took my newly transformed business with me, but my fragile state and ungrounded energy brought it to a halt. I tried to quickly ground myself in a new place with a new relationship and a completely new lifestyle. Before I could even settle in, I was pregnant. My son joined me earth side in 2020 to be the catalyst I needed to embody the mother archetype and show the f*ck up for both of us. Since then, my world has exploded, all in good ways of course.

My journey to motherhood was nothing like I had ever imagined it would be. I experienced a very unsupported pregnancy, traumatic birth, and postpartum during a pandemic. I also faced motherhood as a single mom. I was left with many layers of deep healing to do as a result and spent my first year postpartum healing and exploring the wounds that surfaced. This gave me crystal clarity in how I could support mothers in ways that go so much deeper than doula support.

As a doula, I already knew that motherhood generally tends to bring up a lot for women. It often unearths childhood traumas as well as issues involving worthiness and empowerment, and many women find themselves face to face with their mother wounds. I had done much of that healing earlier in life, but there are layers that can only be done in motherhood itself, and I found the healing runs even deeper when you're essentially coparenting with your own mom!

I quickly became overwhelmed as I was constantly pulled in different directions. I needed to heal, but my baby needed me. I needed to take care of myself as well as the house and meals. I needed to address the shadows that were coming up. I also needed to figure out how to support myself and my son as a single mom. So, I needed a plan.

I tuned into myself, my needs, my son's needs, and how my body felt. I leaned into my support system, and I continued growing it in areas that needed more attention. I used my voice, asked for help, shared how I felt and what I needed. I remained open, conscious, and aware and I did the work to heal my shadows. I prioritized sacred self-care and I showed up for it even when it was hard. I figured out how to budget my time, balance my energy, and sustain it all. I showed up for my son by showing up for myself every single day.

I embodied the mother archetype, and it has changed my entire life experience. I'm now able to show up as my highest self consistently. I have everything I need to be able to grow, flourish, and prosper. I'm present and in tune with my son, fulfilled in my work and practices, and capable of maintaining a balance. I also surrender to the ebb and flow of life, knowing that I won't feel like, "Yeah, I've got this!" every day. I do struggle sometimes, but I'm aware that healing, growth, and embodiment is not a linear path and I have the tools necessary to easily find equilibrium. Being able to fully show up day in and day out for myself, my practices, and my child in a satisfying way is true embodiment.

Living as an embodied mama has helped me realize that before becoming a mom and going through my own transformative healing journey, I wasn't showing up for myself. I was unable to be present in the ways that are nourishing, consistent, and fulfilling. I was regularly moving through the motions of things that were supposed to help me, but not giving things my all or doing things in a way that would actually make a difference in my life. I refused to make necessary changes and put in the extra effort it required to live the life I desired. To this day, I joke with my first business coach that in order for me to stop resisting some of the pieces of advice she offered, she needed to have given me a kid! Because, for me, *that* is what I needed to really show the f*ck up.

The mother archetype is an energy or spirit that encompasses qualities and characteristics that you'd find in the ideal mother: loving, generous, abundant, caring, kind, and compassionate. She is fertile, strong, and wise. The ultimate mother is our planet Earth who nurtures, nourishes, and sustains us.

The mother archetype is the energy and spirit of *sustaining*. To sustain life—your own as well as a child's—is the true essence of the mother energy. She allows life to thrive in its own right, understanding her part in the natural cycle of things. She knows when to foster growth and when to offer freedom. The mother embodies presence, attention, and care. She is attuned to her child's needs, understanding how best to nurture them because she is fully present with them. But she is also in tune with herself and her own needs, able to care for herself or seek the necessary support to do so. She knows that in order to be present in motherhood, she must be present within herself.

This often goes against one's beliefs of how a mother "should" act, because American society has taught us that as mothers, we should take care of our children first, even at the expense of sacrificing ourselves. The inherent lack of support for moms sets them back from thriving from the very beginning and further perpetuates societal expectation for them to immediately "snap back" and return to normal life. This is damaging and greatly increases the amount of guilt, shame, and feelings of failure new mothers experience. This societal pressure is detrimental to the foundations of motherhood. How can we truly sustain our children's energy, health, wellness, and life? We have to sustain our own.

We see it a lot in stories and movies, the mother runs ragged, giving every last ounce of herself to her children, and possibly even her life in the ultimate sacrifice. Mothers must give a lot, but it doesn't have to be at such an expense. Our planet certainly won't do that! It becomes an issue when mothers give every ounce of their time, energy, and life force until they are left empty and exhausted with nothing left to offer. We also see stories of mothers whose every activity is wrapped up in their child's life somehow. When mothers lose their entire identity to motherhood, they can't let go when necessary. A constant series of letting go is the journey of motherhood; it's part of the process.

It's vital for women not to lose themselves in motherhood. When "mama" isn't your sole identity you're able to embrace all aspects of your life. You're able to grow individually, emotionally, and spiritually. You're able to heal on all levels. You're able to work on yourself, fill your cup and have even more to offer others. It increases your ability to be attuned to your own needs as well as everyone around you. It allows you to be present in your body and in the moment with your family.

The idea of caring for yourself first does not mean neglect your children or responsibilities and only focus on yourself. There is always a balance. We must find that balance and *sustain* it. This energy prevents us from neglecting our children as well as ourselves. Finding the equilibrium can be a struggle sometimes; we may feel that taking time for ourselves or prioritizing our needs is selfish and experience guilt as a result. This is when we might reflect on why we aren't valuing our wellbeing. After all, the wellbeing of our children is founded upon our own. We can find a way to embody it that feels good so we can show up every single day. This requires us to tune in with ourselves and find out what we truly need, then take care of our own needs first.

I encourage sacred self-care, not just self-care. It's important not to just use "zen" to numb out. Sacred self-care is not glamorous; it's hard work and includes facing tough shadows. To embody the mother archetype, you must be willing and able to go within and face whatever is there. You must stay connected with your true self and take time to be with yourself, both the dark and the light, to care for and nurture your wounds. The darkness that you might find when going within will require you to do the deep healing you've been avoiding, pushing aside, or are simply unaware of. Shadow work is essential to anyone's soul evolution, but it is highlighted in motherhood. Children are mirrors and they want you to do the work. Inner child struggles, mother wounds, and trauma will all surface. In order to become whole, happy, and present in motherhood, you need to address them. This fills you up, allowing you to be rejuvenated, balanced, and able to not only give more but also handle more of life's plot twists with ease.

Being stuck in our own survival patterns prevent us from experiencing life as our highest self. It keeps us repeating cycles perpetually, and allows life to pass us by if we're incapable of being present in the moment. For instance, there are many moms who make sure basic needs are met, seemingly doing all the right things, but aren't actually present. They're off in their head, lost on their phone, and not grounded in the moment. They may be desperately seeking a mental break by checking out in the ways they are able, lost in work, unable to set and hold boundaries, perpetuating the cycle of the unavailable parent that they experienced, or even so wrapped up in their own survival that they can't see the impact on those around them.

That sort of mom reflects how I was living before motherhood, before embodying the mother archetype. On the surface they meet the requirements, but they aren't present. Before motherhood, I did all the things prescribed in order to achieve success, but I wasn't truly embodying them. You can say all the things, know all the things, and even do all the things, but until you show the f*ck up and embody them, they won't make a difference.

Embodying the mother archetype goes far beyond being caring and nurturing. It means you exude this energy and your default settings are tuned toward inner knowing, attunement, and alignment. You are fully present in your life and thriving in all aspects.

As we embody this energy, sacred self-care becomes a non-negotiable in our routine, resulting in far less overwhelm. Practices and rituals may include adequate healthy sleep, nourishing foods, and routine exercise. We may use embodiment practices to release and heal trauma, especially any birth trauma. Connecting with mother Earth, her elements, and all of her wisdom she has to share with us is a great self-care practice. Ideally, we'll still be able to enjoy practices such as journaling, yoga, meditation, and other yummy rituals we may have indulged in before motherhood, but it also will often look much different. Our self-love practices and rituals may be as simple (or as difficult) as a hot cup of coffee, a hot meal, or exercising with our children. The keys are intention, awareness, and presence. Across the board, general time alone is necessary for mothers. Everyone needs something different regarding self-care and specific practices, so even time alone will vary in terms of the amount needed.

Overall, in motherhood, mothers benefit greatly and feel more capable, balanced, and happy when they are not the sole caregiver day in and day out. Part of embodying this energy is implementing systems of support, which include other people just as much as it includes the tools in our toolbox that support us. I had a birth experience that required me to go outside of myself to give birth. In our society, we are encouraged to not need anybody else, ever, but without outside help, my birth outcome would have been devastating. That experience humbled me and made me surrender to the fact that we cannot and should not do it alone. There is a sense of pride in being able to do so—but if we're not careful, that pride will take over to the detriment of ourselves and our children. There is no shame in asking for or receiving help and support. This is a huge block many mothers need to work through, but if we can do it all alone, imagine what we can do with support!

Embodiment looks different for everyone. Practices, rituals, and even the amount of alone time that each of us needs will change as we, and our children, grow. But with a heap of resources, tools, and practices we will always able to tune in and reflect, heal, transmute, alchemize, and integrate the lessons, as well as get energized, feel great, and sustain life. That's the embodiment of the mother archetype, that's the truth of tapping into the spirit and energy of the mother.

What I learned in my embodiment is this: self-care is not selfish, or a luxury—it is a necessity. I must show up for myself like never before so that I can show up in the ways I need to for my child to grow up happy, healthy, and whole. Motherhood has pushed me to a new level that allows us both to thrive. While motherhood may be what motivates you as well, the transformative work of healing the mother wound, breaking painful patterns and cycles, and embodying the mother archetype can be done at any point in life. You can embody the mother archetype without being a mom and apply this energy to your life and work in the same ways I have.

Legacy to me isn't just building a successful business or raising my son to be a noble man. It's the impact I'll leave behind for women and the seven generations that follow them. I'm empowering women to thrive in life and motherhood by embodying the mother archetype, healing patterns, cycles, and traumas, and showing the f*ck up for themselves. I guide them to face their shadows, transmute and integrate them, and live intentionally. When we are conscious of our wounds, we are aware of triggers, and empowered with choice. The women I work with are learning how to be present with their children, and live life as whole, happy, and healed mamas.

I want every mother to feel seen, heard, and supported. While ideally we'd live in a society that doesn't need to ask or be told how to support moms, I want every mom to know she is never alone; she must only speak up for herself, show up for herself, and create her experience and legacy. Every mama needs to know that her child's success begins with her. The most important thing we can do for our children and their role in our legacy is to be fully present with them and thrive in motherhood. So, we all need to show the f*ck up. Show up for yourself. For your children. Embody the mother archetype to sustain life and thrive.

ABOUT THE AUTHOR
HEATHER ROBINSON

Heather Robinson is a mother and the founder of Embodied Mamas. She mentors mothers to thrive in all aspects of life by embodying the mother archetype. Through prioritizing sacred self-care and deep wound healing, Heather empowers women with the tools they need to consistently show up as their highest self. Her mission is to ensure the next seven generations have healed, happy, whole mamas who are fully present and in tune with their children.

Embodied Mamas is a natural extension of Heather's own life. She is raising her son, Jasper, in alignment with her values and prioritizing well-being as a means to serve him. This embodiment of her higher self allows her to show up for her son as well as her clients in a holistic and supportive way. She lives in Virginia with her son and rescued cat, Phoenix.

Website: www.iamhro.com
Instagram: www.Instagram.com/iam_hro
Facebook: www.Facebook.com/embodiedmamas

Facebook Group: www.Facebook.com/groups/embodiedmamas
Email: hro.nicole@yahoo.com

13

JANA BARTLETT ALONSO

LESSONS FROM MY DYING MOTHER

Where to start with a story that has so many layers, after so much learning? Usually you would say at the beginning, but in this case I am not sure where the beginning is, and actually it is impossible to know. What I can tell you is that this is the story of a mother and a daughter, and all of the women and men that preceded her. This is a story about our ancestors, as much as it is a story about us and everybody who is alive right now. This is a story about my mother and I, the woman I have loved more than anyone else I have ever known, and the woman who almost broke my heart by leaving this planet too soon, and yet at the perfect time.

I grew up in a little village outside Norwich called Spooner Row. My life was pretty "normal" until I turned nineteen and everything exploded and came flooding out. And by "normal", I mean, it looked normal from the outside, as though everything was going well. You know how we have a tendency to pretend because we don't know any other way? I went to a good school, performed well, was slim and pretty, had boyfriends, and earned top grades.

I did everything you are told you have to do to be successful in this world, and I did it well. Until, at the age of nineteen, in the space of a month, I was diagnosed with depression, anxiety, and an eating disorder. My mum was also diagnosed with Stage 4 cancer. My world collapsed, and everything that had felt safe suddenly did not. I remember being shocked by my mother's illness. This only happened in movies; this only happened to other people, not to me. It's funny, the lies we tell to protect ourselves from the pain of what is real and human. We all have to die, even though we pretend that we don't.

At that time, there were seemingly endless diagnoses, and somehow all of the secrets started coming out as well. I found out that my mother had experienced her first breakdown at nineteen, and ever since then had struggled with overwhelm and depression. This was news to me, as we had always been told that this was just how mum was. I also found out that my mother had struggled with suicidal thoughts, and whilst pregnant with me she had wanted to take her own life. In her third trimester, she was given antidepressants to help her in the final months of pregnancy. This meant that I had also taken antidepressants before even leaving the womb. For this, my mother carried a lot of guilt, so it's important to me to make it clear that she wasn't to blame. She did the best she could, based on what she knew, and maybe she actually saved both of our lives. Out of love for her unborn child, my mother didn't commit suicide all those years ago, and for that I will always be grateful.

What is interesting is that it seems I was born with my mother's pain, her problems with food, and her overactive stress-response and suicidal thoughts. I stopped eating properly as a little girl and was on medication by the age of nineteen, just like my mother had been. Patterns were repeating themselves. What I didn't know then was that this would be the making of me. This would propel me down a track I could have never imagined. And I definitely didn't know that, nine years later, I would be grateful. What I also didn't understand then was that this observation of the pattern would heal me, save me, and that the pain my mother had been carrying would be the catalyst for my transformation.

In the nine years since that month of continuous diagnoses, my mother got better twice, until she got worse again and passed away in July of 2019. But not before she changed our lives. Her experience with cancer and mental health made me a better person, my father turned into the softest and strongest man I know, and my sister's heart broke and then she blossomed in front of my eyes. In her passing, my mother brought us even closer together, and taught us how to live in a completely different way, as if it all counted. Because it does, all of it, not just the stuff we like. She taught us how deeply beautiful and deeply soul-shockingly painful it is to be alive. My mum's story has a happy and an unhappy ending, and this is the duality of life. Both endings are true in their own conflicting ways.

The unhappy ending to this story, the most heart-breaking thing in the world, was that my mum died believing that life was suffering. In the months prior to her death, I used to speak to her about reincarnation, and she used to respond that she hoped it wasn't true because she couldn't bear to go through so much again. My mother had spent her whole life doing what she thought she *should* do. She had raised two kids, worked hard at the university, was a good wife, mother, friend, colleague, and kept going even when she was exhausted and burnt out. She believed the lie of the superwomen who could do it all, and it took away her vitality and health. For her, life was the service of others, and she forgot about herself; she wasn't able to heal her childhood wounds, nor the ones that were passed down. She held trauma in her body from many stories that were never told, and the pain seemed too great to even comprehend. Mum died believing that she was a failure because she had never "done" anything with her life. Another lie we are told is that we have to "do" something; we cannot simply be alive in who we are.

The happy ending to this story is that before she passed, she came to peace with her life, her decisions and the way everything had worked out. She made peace with her death, and left me with the message that it is okay to die—that you can leave in peace. The nurses were astounded by my mother's peace, telling me it was not at all common. We didn't hold on, and nor did she. This is a whole story of its own, but for now I will share with you my father's words to me after she passed: "*Jani, that was a good death. I feel mum just taught us how to die with grace.*" And my body tingled with truth. In teaching me how to die, my mother had taught me how to live.

Her legacy, and what I want to pass on to you, is twofold. The two elements are actually ironically connected—a juxtaposed metaphor for life. First, she taught me that there is much healing work to be done. If we don't deal with the wound, it is passed down from generation to generation, and that is why I have carried my mother's pain. Secondly, even if we don't heal, even if the worst happens and it is our turn to die, it is okay. You can die in peace, with grace, regardless. There is no right or wrong, every experience is valid, and you cannot fail life. You cannot fail experience; it is simply here to teach us. My legacy is a continuation, honoring my mother's life, to share with you what I have learned from her life experience. Look to heal your generational wounding, break the patterns of those before you, and write a different story. All experience is worthwhile, and if we learn from it, anything can be healed and changed. You are not to blame for whatever happens in your life, but you are responsible for it. Understanding this can change your whole existence.

'Generational wounding' isn't simply a woo-woo concept talked about in shamanic medicine, even though they understood much more that we have yet to comprehend. It has now been proven by science, and I am not talking about genetics, cancer genes, addiction genes, or mental health genes. Epigenetics is a growing field of science that focuses on how life-experiences influence genes, and in turn us, our behaviours and patterns. It describes how environments create disease and maladaptive patterns within. Bruce Lipton, the famous cell biologist writes: "The cell's operations are primarily molded by its interaction with the environment, not by its genetic code."

These findings point to the prenatal and early childhood environment as crucial to how a child develops. This is how wounding is passed down. For example, if you have a very stressed and fearful mother, this has an impact on her child's development, how their brain develops, and who they become in the world. Studies have shown ($^1/^2$) that maternal stress or anxiety during pregnancy can affect the child in various ways, such as an increased risk of learning difficulties, the creation of behavioral and emotional patterns associated with addiction, and an increased likelihood of anxiety and fearfulness in their lives. A stressed mother means higher levels of cortisol which is harmful to brain structures, especially in times of rapid development.

Studies[3] have shown that some women who suffered PTSD after the 9/11 attacks passed on these effects to their children. Even at the age of twelve months, these children still had abnormal levels of cortisol. Children with stressed mothers during pregnancy are more likely to have disturbed stress-control mechanisms over the long-term. They are also more likely to have a scarcity of dopamine receptors responsible for happiness, motivation, and pleasure. This leads to stress, fear, and bodily responses being passed down through generations.

As you can imagine, I was a stressed child, and I have been a stressed adult. Just like my mother, I notice how easily I become overwhelmed and how I cope less well than others, and regulate myself less well too. I was also fearful as a child. I cried when my parents put me down. I was anxious and wanted to be held, or completely left alone. Now that I understand epigenetics, it isn't surprising that I stopped eating properly at seven and was diagnosed at nineteen. My brain development was disturbed before I was even born.

But where did her pain come from? I believe that it wasn't hers—it was passed down, from generation to generation. You see, my mother was born after the Spanish Civil War. My family were Spanish refugees in Morocco, and her childhood was filled with stories of fear and running away from Spain. Her granddad used to tell her repeatedly how her grandmother had been shot, killed and thrown into a mass grave when she was eight months pregnant. She was raised on stories of fear about Franco and how terrible this world can be. My grandmother's favorite activity around the dinner table is to tell us how unfair life is: "If there was a God, it wouldn't be like this." But can we blame her? She was born into war, lost her parents, then flew to Morocco alone at fourteen to meet her father for the first time. More recently, she lost her daughter, husband and sister within a year and half, but she is still here, strong and present, loving and kind. So, is she to blame? No, she has done the absolute best she can in a life that hasn't been easy.

My great-grandfather isn't to blame either. No one is. We are all humans doing our best, and sometimes we are put into terrible situations where our focus is on survival alone. What is important is to see how war and world events affect whole generational lines that become stuck in a heightened stress response: survival mode. It is then essential to learn how to shift out of survival mode to stop this trauma from being passed down. This is what I teach. Learning how to escape survival mode has been the primary focus of my healing journey. It is also what I have found hardest.

It is also important to note that trauma isn't only passed through physical responses and epigenetics, but through beliefs. My grandfather had a core belief that life was suffering, my grandmother tells me the same thing all of the time, and it was one of the final things my mother told me before she died. What we hear as a child becomes a neurological truth; the beliefs of the adults around us easily become programmed & memorized in a child's highly plastic brain. That is where the real work is, to identify what is in our unconscious mind and let go of the beliefs that don't serve us in our life. I was fortunate to have a father who loved life. His motto was that everything happens for a reason and there is often a silver lining. That core belief has carried me through anything difficult in my life. My dad also taught me that I could do anything. All I had to do was put one foot in front of the other. I like to call these "protective beliefs", and I truly believe they pulled me out of my depression.

Beliefs and thought patterns are passed down through generations, almost like stories that we tell one another about the world. Each family has beliefs about money, relationships, life, love, commitment and beyond. Some of these stories are healthier than others; some create illness, yet some create health. When you become an adult, your work is to question everything your family has taught you and every belief you hold, and assess if it is nourishing or harmful. Ask yourself:

Is what I am telling myself truly true?

Does this belief create the world and life I desire?

If it doesn't, what does my heart actually yearn for?

It is possible to reprogram the beliefs that have been passed down your generation line. This is *powerful* healing work that can completely transform your life.

If you are reading this, you have an opportunity to heal what those who came before you couldn't. This work isn't to blame them for their beliefs and bodily responses. The work is to see where *you* can take responsibility, heal and break the pattern. You have the power to change the narrative your family has been living. You have the power to change your narrative. My mother always used to tell me, without knowing any of the science, "Jani, you seem to be healing what I couldn't." And she was right. My work, my legacy, is to heal as much as I can, so I don't pass it down to my children. It is impossible to heal everything and mistakes happen; this knowledge holds learning and self-compassion. Whatever I can't heal, they can; it becomes their turn. And so on, we keep going. This is the process of an eternal healing-line.

My mother will live within me forever; her life will guide me for as long as I'm on this earth, and one day I will tell my daughters about her. I will tell them about how she laughed, how she lit up a room, how she was made of pure stardust that attracted everyone to her, magnetic, with love. I will tell them how she used to sing along with The Pogues at Christmas, and "How much is that doggy in the window" for the rest of the year, simply because they gave her joy. My mother was unique and completely herself. I used to think that the world wasn't ready for her. I now see my mother was misunderstood. She pushed too hard for too long, and abandoned herself trying to make herself fit into a society that is unhealthy. She held beliefs that didn't serve her. Deep down, she was scared, and forgot herself by looking after everyone around her. She used up all of her energy before she was 60 years old, and her body could no longer cope. She was caught in an overactive stress-response and her depression was not understood.

I will also teach my children my mother's final words, and the wisdom she gathered during the final days of her life, when she found peace:

"Don't get lost in noise, Jani. Everything you think is important right now isn't as essential as you think it is."

"When you are dying, you realize that all of those people you have been worrying about don't even enter your mind."

"Keep it simple, darling—simplify."

"I have realized that life is just about eating a peach and truly being there, and that's it."

"You know, Jani, dying isn't as bad as I thought it would be."

You see, wounds and beliefs aren't the only things passed down ancestral lines. There is also love, wisdom gained, and memories made. You can't fail life. All you can do is live the best way you can for the years that you are given, and rejoice in every day gifted to you on this planet.

1. M.J. Meaney, " Maternal Care, Gene Expression, and the Transmission of Individual Differences in Stress Reactivity Across Generations,"
2. . P. Zelkowitz and A. Papageorgiou, "Maternal Anxiety: An Emerging Prognostic Factor in Neonatology,"
3. R. Yehuda et al., "Transgenerational Effects of Posttraumatic Stress Disorder in Babies of Mothers Exposed to the World Trade Center Attacks During Pregnancy,"

ABOUT THE AUTHOR

JANA BARTLETT ALONOSO

Jana is an English-Spanish Integrative Healing Expert. She teaches people to become self-healers and the alchemists of their own existence, so they can transform pain into pleasure, trauma into triumph, and blockages into blessings. She believes that only by shedding and facing our wounds we can rise and create the authentic lives that we truly desire.

In 2020, after nearly 10 years of study and experience, she birthed the school of Integrative Healing while taking people on 1:1 journeys of self-exploration. She uses an integrative approach and works with multiple modalities to teach women to transform their relationships, work through their subconscious patterns, behaviors and blockages, reconnect with their pleasure, and learn to listen to their bodies signals. Her greatest passion is teaching women to truly understand trauma and emotions and heal from their previous experiences. Jana now lives and works in the mountains of Malaga.

Websites: www.alonsojana.com

www.alonsojana.com/integrative-healing/
Instagram: www.instagram.com/janabartlettalonso
Facebook: www.facebook.com/Integrative-Healing-
1999278676850865
Email: info@janaintegrativehealing.com

14
JESSICA TORRES

SEX WITH GOD

There is no better sex than the sex you'll have with God. You can rave about your multi-orgasmic intercourse with your lover, your body quivers, your slow motion cervical rapture, and it will come very, very, very close...but it will always end. There will always be a point where it's time to go back to life. To work, to kids, to jobs, to commitments, and so on. The sex that never ends isn't the sex we've been told about, or shown, or the kind we do with one another behind closed doors. This is a different kind of sex. A different kind of merging. That doesn't involve you having to take your clothes off and getting warmed up to orgasm. This is the path of the heart. It's about opening your perception a little wider to experience the depth of the erotic God in mundane life. What makes sex with God the best sex we'll ever come to experience is that it is weaved into the greatest love you'll ever know—and there is no ending. Ever. It is eternally hot. There is also no beginning. We've been having sex with God our whole lives whether aware of it or not.

I know you're probably already dripping, but this chapter is not going to be as gushing as this first paragraph. I'm going to share with you my experiences getting to this space and relationship with God. This is my ever-evolving legacy.

Like many women, my number one fantasy is to be chosen. To be in love, desired, and wanted by another. To be continuously chosen in a way like when we hear the words, "That's her. That's my girl. I love her so much. I choose her, forever." And if this isn't a fantasy for you, I invite you to tap into your inner child, your inner teenager, or the feeling that occurred within your body when you experienced that first heartbreak from the boy you had a major crush on when he told you he liked another girl. That feeling beyond rejection, abandonment and betrayal. That feeling of not being fully seen for the beauty that you really are and know yourself to be in your heart.

The idea of this love was always thought to have to come from another. All I ever really wanted was myself. Was love for myself, onto myself, by my self. I just did not know. I was never modeled or shown an example of someone who was in a healthy, secure relationship with themselves. I was raised in a home where there was emotional enmeshment and lack of clear communication. In my teens, I was living in a home where there was no sexual boundaries and I was never told of the sacredness in sex. Or that a relationship with God could be beautiful. I was shown that God was church and scripture, boring and unnecessary. And stale.

The truth about me and my journey is that I am an incest survivor. And I don't use the word 'survivor' for you to feel pity for me, but rather to express to you that this has actually brought me to death by dissociation. Death without leaving the Earth. Leaving my body without leaving the 3D plane. Death of a healthy psyche. Although incest created much somatic trauma in my body, most of the trauma was done to my mind. The patterns and behaviors that stemmed from sexual encounters with a sibling. The shame, the guilt, the confusion, the lust, the love, the enticement, the comfort, the pleasure and the pain. I have died. I have left my body. From all of this. But it did not happen from actually leaving this earth. The leaving and dissociation all happened while still being here.

Up until recent years, I always felt like 'the girl from the broken home.' Out of my closest friends when I was a teen, I was the only one who didn't go to bed at night with two parents in the master bedroom. I remember being on vacation with my friend's family when I was twelve or thirteen, and I cracked a joke at her brother. He responded with something along the lines of, "What do you know? You're from a broken home." And that f*cking cut me. I remember my heart swelling and wanting to instantly bawl my eyes out. Instead I played it cool, laughed it off, acted like it didn't bother me, and walked away swallowing down what felt like mounds of dirt mixed with broken glass. My depth of emotional intelligence was activated and carved out because I was from a 'broken' home. And I hung on to that story for years and let it run my life in a destructive direction. I became addicted to the pain. My belief was that I'd always struggle. I'd always be broken. And there was no sense trying because my roots were already tainted. Who was I but a girl from a broken home?

In my youth, I polarized my pain with overachievement, until dancing with the devil felt like way more fun. And so I began to use numbing and escaping to get those instant hits of dopamine to distract myself from the well of pain I had yet to feel from all of the unprocessed emotions I swallowed to keep my spine straight. It wasn't safe for me to fall apart back then. At least, I didn't know that it was possible to fall apart without completely dying and being laid to rest. Rock bottom for me was in my early twenties. A time when I was heavily addicted to Adderall, saying yes to relationships that felt more like self-betrayal, selling my body for money, and having no sense of direction as to where my life was going. Ironically, this is when I had my first, conscious, taste of God's sweet love.

If we fast forward to now, how did I move from this pain to living my dream reality? It was not so long ago I was living in my dysfunctional family home, overcome by a scarcity mindset. I worked forty hours a week in a restaurant—and I was good at it. I wouldn't be who I am today if I had never served those years in the industry. But it started getting to this point where my God-given gifts were not able to thrive in the environments that I was choosing for myself. Something had to change. My body told me so. My heart told me so. And I began to activate the universe with my desire for this dream reality I saw myself waking up to.

And then, my prayer was answered. One day, I was crossing the street near the restaurant I worked at, and a car was headed towards me. Inside the car happened to be a woman who I was connected with through mutual friends. This woman was an angel for me. She was two years into her own online business, which was supporting other women in starting their own soul-aligned businesses. Before this encounter, I never asked for help. For one, I was much too prideful in that lone wolf mentality, and secondly, I did not know how to ask for help. I was conditioned to think I had to do it all alone. Until the mirror reflection of this woman created a response in my body that nearly screamed "HIRE HER". I had no idea what I was getting myself into. But I listened and joined her online group program to receive guidance on starting my own business. This was a crucial time in my life. I began showing up on my platform in ways I had always dreamed of. I began expressing myself and unraveling limited beliefs and stories that had been running my life for years. I began trusting myself and my God channel.

At this time, I was also newly engaged to my high school sweetheart and my life was pretty much planned out for me. I was in denial about this life with this man not being the vision I had in my heart. Yet, I said yes for comfortability and security. I was in too deep. That all changed as I was nearing the end of this group program when I went on a solo trip to Costa Rica for a retreat with my coach and some of her other clients. The retreat set my soul on fire. I felt so high and everything in my life was perfect. Until it wasn't.

After the retreat, a few of us traveled to the city for a couple days. The night we got there we were brought to a mutual friend's gorgeous apartment for a night of connection. That night, I was introduced to a man who, for the first time in a long time, made me feel extremely turned on. The night progressed and I began to open more to him. The conversation and depth that he embodied was incredibly attractive. The charge began to ignite. The presence that he offered me made me feel like a Goddess. I had never felt this way around a man before. We went out dancing that night and this man and I clearly had an attraction for each other. And something within me was hooked. On him. I wanted it. I wanted him. And there, in Costa Rica, I cheated on my fiancé with this man I had just met.

I remember the feeling in my body on the plane ride home. I clutched my mala beads. I chanted to Ganesh to support me in this obstacle that I was about to face. I knew what I had to do. I knew that it was going to propel me into another reality. Maybe not consciously, but subconsciously there was a force that moved me and had been supporting me all along. I trusted it. And I did just that. Within hours of coming home from my trip, I told my fiancé about my infidelity. He took the ring back.

This trauma brought to the forefront all of the sexual trauma I had experienced in my childhood. What was coming up for me was so much more than my emotional body at the time could handle, and I had my entire family telling me that I was bi-polar, schizophrenic and needed help. The grief was unbearable. My heart was being cracked open in a way that I had never experienced before. And there was a certain separation happening. It was a certain initiation from being in an emotionally enmeshed, codependent, dysfunctional family into a sovereign adult with healthy boundaries and secure relationship dynamics. I felt like a foreigner in my own home. I felt like I had no one outside of myself to turn to that would receive me, emotionally.

I began to turn within. I began to date myself. I began to dance, a lot. And although my dream of having my own online business was at the forefront of my vision, I knew that what I had to be putting my energy into in the moment was my healing in its entirety. And that holding this space for myself right now would open me up to in turn hold space for others. I began doing things I've never done before that both pushed me to the edges of where I was comfortable and excited me. I would take myself on dates to ecstatic dances in New York City. I would take myself to five rhythms classes and express myself in way I never have. I would say yes to every exciting opportunity that came my way. I began hosting free online ecstatic dance and spoken word gatherings from my platform where people would show up and we'd express ourselves together.

There is something else I started to do during this time. I was allowing myself to grieve. I was single. I had no job. Not much money. I experienced missed opportunities, estranged relationships with family members, terrible bouts of grief, and depression and anxiety. Every single limiting belief came up. The moment I would wake up, the story of unworthiness would play in my head. I was questioning my mental health, and my entire existence. I gave in to my self-sabotaging tendency to overeat, my skin broke out, and I shamed myself for all of it. I had terrible regrets for the choice that got me to that point. I felt so embarrassed and guilty. Residual anger from the repressed past sexual traumas that I had no idea were inside of me were coming up to be screamed about. Then began the whole cycle of shaming myself for not being healed yet after doing this work for years. My heart was cracking open. One day I'd be up. The next day, I'd be down. I was becoming an excellent surfer of my own emotional waters. Expansion and contraction. My practice became almost obsolete during this time. I couldn't meditate, pray, breathe, journal, sing, or even dance it away. Although all of these things relieved my suffering, I had to feel it completely and surrender to the reality of my actions. I allowed myself to fully be in my humanity. I allowed these old selves to die. The waves began to subside and I felt this newfound sense of intimacy with life.

And just after this is when it happened. One night, in the depths of my despair, I had made plans to reconnect with a man who I had met years earlier, and through synchronicity we were brought back in contact with each other. I had no intentions of getting into another relationship. Yet, after that first night, the electrical charge formed. God pulled us together, like magnets. Similarly, he was at a point in his life where he was healing from traumas. We immediately laid it all out on the table with each other. It felt so safe to express to each other. He accepted me when I expressed to him my recent infidelities and betrayals. I felt so seen. From that point on I didn't feel so alone on this journey. Michael supported me in my sovereignty. In holding and setting boundaries with my family. He shared with me so many deeper forms of healing that I had yet to dive into. He would play the guitar for me and I would sing along. He mirrored to me self-trust and radical self-ownership. He didn't give in to my wounded feminine codependency. And best of all, the vision he had for his life was a reflection of mine. And what we decided next was a game changer for us both.

Michael and I had a plan to become digital nomads together. We made large investments in ourselves and hired business coaches. I began showing up on my platform again to continue watering the seeds I had planted the previous summer. I was building momentum under the dream reality vision. By the end of the summer, we moved across the country from New York to Oregon with all of our belongings that we chose to keep in a U-Haul. I was leaving behind everything that was familiar. Just before leaving, I signed my first high-paying client. I trusted that more were coming. And they did. We ran our businesses from our apartment in Oregon for three months. I held my first masterclass and got a taste of what it was like to actually be able to take care of myself financially. And then, the calling came. After two months in Oregon, we decided to move to Costa Rica.

And here we are. I've been running my business from the Caribbean Coast of Costa Rica with my beloved sacred masculine partner. We have manifested a gorgeous home just minutes from the clear blue ocean. We have met the most incredible, beautiful human beings. I've been hitting consistent five-figure months in my business and my clients, who live all over the world, feel like soul sisters.

Every day, I feel chosen. By God. My relationship with God is utterly erotic. I am so turned on. To life. To creating. To love. My relationship with God is what has healed my relationship with myself. My relationship with God has liberated me from self-abandonment and self-neglect in my quest for love from those who were never able to receive the being I am. I yearn to be made love to by God. I yearn to be opened and penetrated by divine white light consciousness so that I could drip and overflow my love onto everything that enters my path. Co-creating with God is my favorite sex position. I am used for God's pleasure as an artist for his consciousness to erect the world. My body is she, the Goddess. I am a vessel for sex magick and the magick itself, all at once. I am no longer concerned with my lower-level desires. I am no longer available for fleeting love. I am here for the infinite, everlasting romance that I feel each time I slow down and tune into my heart. God is right here for me. Saying, "My sweet Love, my sweet child, surrender to me. Trust me. I am never not where you are. Remember the feeling of the space where we merge in intimate communion. The place where time slows down and words fall short. I will be there. Awaiting your sweet love. Eternally."

ABOUT THE AUTHOR

JESSICA TORRES

Jessica Torres is a Sacred Sexuality and Feminine-Based Business Coach and founder of Jessica Torres LLC. Her mission is to turn the world on to the greatest love she has ever known: the love that she has cultivated through her relationship with God. She creates intimate, safe containers to serve her clients while healing sexual and childhood trauma, cultivating a relationship with their bodies, and taking bold action to self-actualize their dreams. Her work is weaved with erotic innocence. Through this embodiment, she is a mirror reflection of love and empowerment for every woman who feels the resonance to work with her. Jessica believes that a relationship with one's inner child is the gateway to living a life of ultimate fulfillment, wonder, beauty, and magick. She is a digital nomad living alongside her partner, running their businesses from wherever in the world they feel called to.

Website: www.iamjessicatorres.com
Instagram: www.instagram.com/imjessicatorres
Email: imjessicatorres@gmail.com

15

JODIE STIRLING

BECOME THE DELIBERATE CREATOR OF YOUR WONDERFUL LIFE!

To: My beautiful family

I have always been a happy, high-vibing, positive person. I was born happy. My mother has told me I was a peaceful, happy baby. I did not cry, and I slept a lot. I spent most of my childhood giggling and saw pleasure in everything. As a child, I was quite shy, although I liked to be around people. Life was simple, and looking back now, I recognize I had a blessed childhood.

Family and friendships were everything to me, and they still are. My brother and I had a wonderful relationship. When we were young, we spent hours playing Lego. We would build cars and take them in the garden and splash about in the swimming pool for hours until our skin was all wrinkled. There were a lot of kids in the street and we would all go off on wonderful adventures together on our bikes. Life was good with him by my side.

My parents divorced and we went our separate ways for a while. He found it exceedingly difficult, while I just accepted it. As we grew into young adults, we came together again and we lived together in our first apartment in Bondi, Australia. What a laugh we would have! We hung out at the beach, went to parties, and travelled to Europe to see our grandparents. We even went on an amazing road trip in the US, starting in New York and ending at Disneyland in California. We laughed the entire way! From walking all those stairs in the Statue of Liberty, standing on the banks at Epcot watching the space shuttle launch, climbing in the Grand Canyon, and visiting Disney, he stood by me. He even saved my hair when a cowboy wanted to cut off my pony tail! Our relationship stayed strong when we met our now partners and started our own families. He was a great uncle to my children. Then it all changed.

We had a major falling-out and it all stopped. He refused to speak to me, refused to have anything to do with me and my children, and my parents were caught in between. That was nearly ten years ago. My heart was broken, and whatever I try to do, nothing works. He has wiped me from his life. We had a simple breakdown in communication, yet to this day I do not exist for him! I have tried many, many times to change this, but nothing will help. I was so sad and after years of trying to sort this out, I have realised that I although I miss him in my life, I needed to start creating the life that I wanted without him. I am very good at seeing the big picture and making good of most situations and the one with my brother is no different. So, with this experience, I have decided to teach my own children the importance of family, friendship and relationships.

Friends would describe me as fun and would make them laugh. I had no idea what I wanted to do when I left school, so I went to college, graduated, and got a job. I found myself in hospitality and so began my life in service as I serviced guests to meet the expectations of their stay.

I trained many young people in the industry. It was great to see them arrive as newbies, fresh from college or university, and then transform themselves into new leaders and managers over the years. I would often tell them my stories of my love for travel and encourage them to do the same. I remember walking down the street in Florence, Italy and hearing my name being called. I looked across the cobbled road and saw two girls frantically waving. I had coached them in Sydney and they had decided to pack their bags and go travelling! They took my advice and I could not have been happier. I listened intently to their stories, and they went on their way. It felt wonderful to have had such an impact on their lives.

My profession took me to various cities in Australia and then over to London and back again. This was my first taste of new cultures and meeting new people. I had stepped out of my comfort zone. Creating a comfort zone is what we feel we must do to have a safe and happy life. However, stepping out of our comfort zones is a way to keep our souls on the move and enable transition, growth and transformation. I have lived in many parts of the world: London, Luxembourg, Lisbon, Sydney, and Hong Kong. With every move, it's like starting my life all over again...new address, new bank accounts, new driver's license, new schools, new friends, new cultures and sometimes languages. It is exciting! I love it! It keeps life interesting. Before I set off on another journey, people would ask, "How do you do it? How do you pack up your family and move to the other side of the world to live in another country?" Oh, I would love to do that !" they would say. I could not understand what the big deal was, and I would tell them to just go for it, get out of your zone and try something new. Doing this with kids in tow is a whole new experience. Not only do I have to think about how you will find the experience, but now I have three little people to consider as well.

I was not aware of how easy I made an adventurous life look. I just thought everyone around me was able to do the same. I did not know then that it is not so easy for most people....

It really was not until I became a mother that the ease with which I approach change became clearer to me. Before this moment, I was doing what everyone else was doing: working, mastering relationships, getting married, etc. I was sitting in my mothers' group, all of us new mums, and they had so much to complain about. I had nothing. I loved every part of being a mother, even the pregnancy. Yes, I had morning sickness and sciatic pain, but it came and went, and I just moved forward. Yes, there were the sleepless nights, sickness and exhausted days, but looking back I could say that I would not change one moment of it. I have been fortunate that I have been able to be there for my children and not have to work full time. I worked from home when needed and had time to be with them. As a mother, you often hear about 'losing your identity'. I did not feel this. I did not want to be identified by my job title, or what I did for a living. I was more than okay with just being called Jack, Ben or Sophie's mum. I would not change it for anything!

Being a mum has been the greatest experience and has brought me so much love and joy. Pain too, but it is like giving birth—you know it happened, but can you still feel it? I know it is not for everyone. I loved to rub it in at events I attended with my husband for his work. There, all the corporate ladies would ask, "What do you do?" I would have great pleasure in saying, "Oh, I am a mum!" They could not relate, and I even had one woman turn her back on me.

It is not always rosy, and the teen years can be challenging, but I have always done the best that I could do at the time. I sometimes reflect on what I could have done better, but realize that at that time I did my best. No regrets just keep moving forward.

I am a great *manifester*.

I didn't even know what that word meant until I was in my forties. I had learned from my father to set goals. I knew about vision boards, but it was not until I had gone through a major shift in my life that I was attracted to *The Secret*, a book written about the Law of Attraction. From that moment, I just got it. I read books, watched movies and I learned how to manifest what I want in life. I told all my friends and family about it, as well as anyone who would listen. I used it to send me where I want to live, what I want to be doing, and the direction I want to go. I was even able to manifest the house I wanted to live in from a photo. It was at that same time that I realized that I needed to have a shift in what I would do with my life.

That is when kinesiology found me. I graduated from a program and set up my own business in a chiropractic clinic in Luxembourg to help children and their parents understand their dominant learning profile. With the use of muscle testing, it is possible to know our dominant ear, eye, brain, hand and foot. You may be surprised at how this can improve your children's learning. Parents of children with conditions such as learning difficulties, sleeping disorders, major stress and bad habits would self-refer to my services because they wanted their child 'fixed'. I did not 'fix' children. I helped children using strategies to develop insight into why they were experiencing these difficulties to give them learning techniques and ways to be responsible for their learning.

This automatically led to them being empowered with being at peace with the way that they are. There are thirty-two different learning profiles, and when you learn something new or under stress, you default to your profile. Once you know yours and each of your family member's, you can understand how best to approach and interact with each other as a family as well as how you absorb information.

One time, a mum brought in her two sons, Charlie and Harry, to see me. At thirteen and twelve years old, the two of them did not get along at all. Their mother could not understand why, and was at her wits' end. When I went through their dominant profiles, it was clear that we were dealing with two totally different children. They were peas from the same pod, but very different. Charlie, the younger of the two, was labelled 'gifted' and 'talented'. He was left brain dominant, very methodical, and used language as his main way of communicating. Harry, the eldest, was right brain dominant and learned best through movement. He was creative, loved anything sporty, and could be loud and boisterous. When I gave their mum these learning profiles and explained how each one worked, she could see exactly what I saw. Charlie needed lots of details, and Harry wanted to run about whilst she talked to him. Charlie totally understood what I was talking about and gave me the greatest analogy to explain their differences. He said, "When Mum asks us if we would like to make a chocolate cake, I listen and get all the ingredients ready to make chocolate cake, and Harry would be setting the table getting ready to eat it". Charlie's dominant brain needs all the information, while Harry's creative brain is already imagining himself sitting down and eating the cake as he needs to chunk the information backwards. This information helped their mum to understand that she needs to explain things to her boys differently, and also come to better understand each other. One month later, there was harmony in the house. Charlie now takes great pride in being gifted and talented, and his mum is okay with Harry having to move while doing his homework. This is also useful for children in the classroom as they learn, for instance, which ear and eye are dominant, so they can sit in the classroom to have full access to the teacher. It is life-changing!

The more I worked with children and their parents, I realized a lot about myself that I did not even know was in me. I love helping people. I seem to attract those who need it.

We know that everything is energy, right? I remember that from science class! One of the greatest scientists ever, Nikola Tesla, said, If you want to find the secrets of the universe, think in terms of energy, frequency and vibration." Albert Einstein also states, "Everything is energy. Match the frequency of the reality you want, and you cannot help but get that reality. It can be no other way. This is not philosophy. This is physics."

With these wise words and other teachers such as Joe Dispenza and Abraham Hicks, it became clear to me that the law of attraction and manifestation was what comes naturally to me. This is how I shape my reality with my mind. What I thought about for my future or what I wanted to do, I could see and feel happening. Just like when I fell in love with a beautiful house in the country, I knew that my family was going to live there. My mind was clear, I had no objections, and would not even allow negative thoughts. This is what I wanted for the future moving forward; I could see it, so it happened. However, I realize that for many this is not the case. If you want to keep moving forward, stop being in the past! The universe has an abundant flow of positive powerful energy. When you align with that loving powerful force of energy, you become a magnet for more of it.

I truly did feel like a magnet. What I set my mind to, I could achieve. I did not let anything set me back. I always had a can-do natural positive attitude to the things I wanted. Therefore, it manifested! Then, last year I found a device that accelerated my manifestation possibilities and my life exploded...

It started with my mother who was suffering with severe sciatic pain. She'd had this pain for years. We were looking for something, anything, that would help her. A little device came into my life which harmonizes the cells to come back into optimal function. This meant that any pain and inflammation my mother was experiencing could be treated with it. It simply restores energy at a cellular level, and you regenerate the very essence of your body. As your cells vibe with power, you start to feel better and live a better life. When you are vibrating on a high frequency, you bring balance to your life energetically, emotionally and mentally. We purchased it, she used it, and she got better and better.

I then started looking into it further and found out that it was invented by a physicist who had been a monk for over a decade. He discovered how to tap into all realities that are possible, and when we focus on things we want, these things start to show up in our lives.

I was blown away. The same device amplified my manifesting which affected everything. My businesses, my friendships, my confidence, and my career contacts. It's been an amazing journey. I am so grateful that this device has come into my life as it makes me feel alive and enriched. I have found y place of love, bliss and joy! I love to share this skill so others can be responsible for their own happiness and joy. you too can become the deliberate creator of your wonderful like!

This year I turned fifty! They say, life begins at fifty. I think they also say it at thirty and forty! With every decade, there is change. My fiftieth year has been real turning point for me. I have always been in awe of people and their stories–they did that! Wow, they took that opportunity when they had nothing! Look at what they have become. Then I realized that I have done that also. I do have a story, but I do not see a sad story. However, it is most definitely a story. It has just become my story of growth and transformation.

With all that I now know, negative people have dropped out of my life and I have been at peace with letting them go. Nothing grows in acidic soil. Negative interactions attract negative relationships. This goes for my brother. If we want positivity, then we must surround ourselves with the right people in the right environment. Moaning about the weather will not change it; just as being sad about something will not make you happy. You are the only person who can change your reality and make it what you want it to be. Always Move forward and take up the opportunities that come your way. It is exciting to have a wonderful shift. Sometimes these skills come naturally. I practice gratitude on a regular basis and have a jar on my kitchen table to remind me to write reasons for gratitude down. My intention is to do this daily and then, at the end of the year, read them and remember all the wonderful things of that year that can quite easily be forgotten in the day-to-day routine. It is important to draw upon them to nourish your soul, especially when you need to be reminded that life is good. Happy reflections bring us to a place of joy.

My children are all grown up and two of them left home for university this year. Although it has been difficult for me to see them leave, it is also exciting to see them start a new life for themselves. We spend so much time teaching them to be decent, kind, loving, empathetic humans and guide them on their journey to adulthood that when they leave, it is both heart-breaking and rewarding that you have helped them to this point. They have a strong value of family that I know will be passed down to their own families. That is what life is about for me as we strive to bring ourselves to a place of greater meaning, joy and positivity that will sustain us. Within my place in the world, I hope to leave an impact on as many people as I can by teaching, empowering, coaching, and guiding the next generation, including my own children. How beautiful would it be for everyone to live out their own life with joy, purpose and happiness so they can guide others to do the same.

ABOUT THE AUTHOR

JODIE STIRLING

Jodie Stirling is a kinesiologist, who lives life to the fullest with frequencies as she is a naturally high vibing human. Her mission is to spark joy and love in humans, help those who suffer with pain and hormonal imbalances, and empower children to be at peace with who they truly are. As an entrepreneur in hospitality, she is passionate about hosting guests and coaching new hosts to be successful and thrive. She is a naturally high-vibing human and a go-getter who tries her hand at everything that comes her way.

Jodie is an Australian living in the UK with her husband, three children, their dog Buddy, and a hive full of bees. Some of her fondest memories are traveling, making new connections and building lifelong memories. Her greatest legacy is to ignite joy in others and enjoy life with her family.

Instagram: https://www.instagram.com/jodie.stirling/
Facebook: https://www.facebook.com/jodie.stirling.9
Email: jodiestirling@gmail.com
Clubhouse: @jodiestirling

16

JULIA RUGO

THE NOTION OF EMOTION

There was an uncontrollable, constant flow of tears falling down my stern and serious face. I would lose it to the emotion every once in a while, releasing audible sounds of my depression and pain. I was fifteen, sitting in the waiting room of my first therapist's office. My mom discussed my condition with the woman inside; I had just met her for the first time. My case was severe. I didn't really think it mattered though. What do my feelings matter? I had been really good at holding it all inside…until it couldn't be held in any longer.

The tears that were here, in the waiting room, had been there, inside the office, and were there, in the car, and there, in the locker room, and even there, in the public halls of my high school. I bustled around, stone-faced, still acing all my honors and advanced placement classes, and teaching myself the lessons since I could barely get out of bed to make it to class. I had great friends, I was a strong athlete, I had a supportive family, and I was smart— but I had been living to please others which led to suppressing myself, my emotions, my sensitivity, my creativity, my feelings.

Anti-depressants were immediately prescribed, along with weekly therapy. Prozac induced feelings of extreme anger, so we tried a few others and settled on Lexapro. I was already on hormonal birth control for two years prior, as I had inconsistent periods and bad acne. Acutane doses came and went without changing much. We added Trazadone and Wellbutrin for my mental health. Some anti-anxiety medicine, too. By college, I was taking more than seven medicines for my mental and hormonal health at once.

I spilled it all in my talk-therapy sessions, because that's what I was there to do, right? Whatever I'm supposed to do, I'd do it. I had always been obedient. So, I talked about how sad I was, the little things that were happening in my life, being overwhelmed, and the mental pain I was in. In more recent years through my healing process, I've discovered what was underneath this pain: unworthiness, extreme lack of confidence, doubt, distrust, disbelief, trauma, and passivity.

By college, I had a new therapist and added a second weekly session of Dialectical Behavioral Therapy (DBT). I began seeing a renowned psychotherapist at a Boston hospital, who mentioned the diagnosis "bipolar" to me.

I hadn't had a manic episode yet, so it was bipolar depression. They still had me on "normal" anti-depressants, and nothing for anti-psychosis. By junior year, the stress and depression was so intense I had to take a semester break from the elite engineering college I was attending. I was studying one of the most demanding majors— Electrical and Computer Engineering in the realm of digital communications through frequency processing. I went back home for outpatient group therapy a few weeks before Christmas.

Therapy, therapy, therapy; medicine, medicine, medicine. It *must* have helped, but there was always a need for more. We never reached the root of the problem, and no medicine or therapy was significantly helping me. There'd be a minor release, and then I'd need a new medicine or a change in medicine. I am a very determined person, so I stayed in school despite my mental illness and other challenges. Sometimes, I would sleep until 9pm at night. Things were getting much worse at this point. I'd sleep more and then I'd sleep less, pulling all-nighters for course-load and project management. I had to reduce the amount of courses I'd take at a time in order to maintain any sanity.

By my fifth year of college, I experienced a traumatic event over the summer—and then I was back to complete my Master Qualifying Project. In essence, it was a senior project where my teammate and I created a touch-learning keyboard device. It lasted a semester and a half, and during this time I went mad.

I would sleep for three days straight. I'd be awake for three days straight. I was not seeing a therapist because I didn't want to. I would stay in the lab all night doing my part of the project. I was on 60+ mg of adderall (for my newly diagnosed ADHD) along with all the other anti-depressants. At 4am, I would research down rabbit holes about "spirit science"— angels and numerology and chakras and yoga. I would consume only tea and green smoothies. All of this lit me up, and I lost over twenty pounds in a few months. I was officially manic.

My own self-awareness woke me up to my mania, though my mother also helped inch me towards this discovery. Watching from the outside, she had read a book which she encouraged me to read called *An Unquiet Mind* by Kay Redfield Jamison, who also suffered from bipolar. I recognized myself in every page...and concluded I was manic-depressed. And this manic episode, my spiritual awakening, was the greatest blessing of my life.

I went to my psychotherapist who I loved, (one I had settled on in my hometown on the shores of New England) and explained to her what had been going on. We changed my medicine to mood-stabilizers paired with anti-psychotics, and I went back to therapy. I also started practicing yoga and daily mindfulness meditation, or *vipassana*.

From my joyful and thrilling research during mania, I understood that there are energy centers inside of my body. From there, I began relating to them and experiencing them through my mental, emotional, and physical states. I saw my mental illness through the eyes of my energy—my crown *chakra* had been burst open. I was infinitely connected to the cosmos and what I know now as transformative energy. I had to bring all the imbalanced energy up in my head, down into my body.

Normally, energy healing works with the chakras from the root (Earth energy) up to the crown (cosmic or divine energy). There are seven primary energy centers in the human body: Root, Sacral, Solar Plexus, Heart, Throat, Third Eye, and Crown. The Root, Sacral, and Solar Plexus (or navel) chakras relate to our Earth self. The Throat, Third Eye, and Crown are our Spiritual self. The Heart is the bridge between the two.

I noticed that my Heart was blocked through my body—my shoulders were extremely hunched over like a protective cage. This came from the walls I had built around it, not trusting the compassion of those around me and completely lacking self-love. I understood I had to break open my heart in order to let the energy through. I chose yoga to help me do this.

My daily yoga practice was simple. It involved sun and moon salutations, balances such as tree pose, and heart openers like sphinx. My meditation practice tuned me into observing my thoughts, my emotions, and how they felt in my body. While sitting, I learned that every emotion passes. At first, the emotions felt worse and more intense when I brought awareness to them. I let myself feel each feeling fully, and I trusted that it would change. The feeling would morph into something new as I had learned from a book on vipassana meditation I had been studying. I might feel anxiety or constriction, and this awareness amplified it. If it became too much to bear, I would return awareness to my breath. There is always something else to focus on, and a new part of the body and associated emotion would speak to me. In time, I would return to that difficult one, and find that it felt more easeful. In time, or a few sits later, I would feel release. My catalyst for healing was actually experiencing that everything changes, even in a micro-nuance, and allowing myself to feel. By experiencing this, I simultaneously built trust in the practice and in myself.

During the year of beginning my yoga and meditation practice, I also attended therapy three times a week. This is why I believe in radical wellness and looking at things from all sides. I encourage being open to a holistic perspective, an energetic perspective, a mental perspective, a physical perspective, and receiving support. Take what feels good, leave what does not, and release judgement. When we release judgement, we first must notice the judgement, so that we can allow it to be released. Our perception of the problem will dictate the outcome.

Through my practice, I noticed my mind and my body starting to change. I felt more peace and motivation. I felt more rooted in myself. I was shifting my vibration through yoga postures (*asana*), chanting the sounds of my chakras (*bīja* mantra), and observing my mind, body and emotions in meditation. Aside from feeling more peaceful, I saw this change most noticeably through my feet. The way I was standing and walking, energetically, had shifted, and showed up through huge, painless, bubble blisters on the soles of my feet. I was *physically* re-wiring my manic-depressive past through the means of energy.

It was extremely potent to notice this change through my feet; they are the root of both the physical body and energetic self. The soles of our feet are like the stalk of a lotus. The pathway of vitality begins here as they connect and anchor to the Earth. This solidified the realness of my subtle body, and vibrational healing. The key to my mind-body-soul connection was here— shifting my vibration through sound, physical posture, and mindfulness.

I knew that I did not want to be on pharmaceuticals any longer. They didn't mesh with my beliefs. From the research I had done and my own spiritual journey, I believed in holistic and herbal-based health. With the help of my psychiatrist, I began to ween myself off of the medicine, deliberately and slowly. Alongside therapy and my yoga/meditation practice, I was able to release the medicine that had been my lifeline for eleven years.

I have been off all anti-depressants and anti-psychotics since 2018, which was three years after the initial manic episode. It was challenging to make the final effort to exit the one sole mood-stabilizer I had reduced myself to, which I was still taking although inconsistently. I was afraid to fully let it go. What if I became crazy? Or depressed, suicidal? I realized it wouldn't break me, now that I had the power and tools to work through my emotions. Now, I manage my stress and what was said to be a medicine-dependent, chronic illness, through mindfulness and my spiritual practices. I feel better than ever and have stepped into my purpose, which has made clear my legacy on this planet.

I believe in healing and transforming from an energetic standpoint: "vibrational healing". Looking at an ailment from the level of vibration will address the root of the problem. Learning about the energetic centers of your body and how they show up in your physical, emotional, mental, and spiritual worlds can absolutely shift your mindset and understanding. The energetic centers affect our external worlds as well, such as career, personal, and social life. The chakra system should be considered and utilized for any physical, mental, or emotional problem.

Why does energy matter? Well…because energy creates matter. Therefore, energy has created us—energy and vibration are the baseline of human-beings and all life. I endured those years in frequency engineering for a reason. I understand the scientific principles behind energy healing. When we learn about, look at, and shift our energy, we can evolve and heal faster. Energy is vibration, similar to how sound is actually a vibrating wave. Our chakras each have a sound, which allows us to tune, enhance, and shift our energy. The postures in a yoga asana practice also balance our chakra centers, allowing the energy to flow and move as we encourage our body to flow and move. Conscious movement paired with conscious breath will shift energetic avenues called "meridians" throughout the body. This allows *prana*, our life force, to flow more freely. Through mindfulness, we can become aware of our emotions and see *what they are telling us.*

I believe in emotional power. When I suppressed my emotion, I had suppressed my creativity, my power, my desires, and became unwell. I was out of touch with myself on every plane. The sacral chakra is the seat of emotion, creativity, and pleasure. Its element is water; it is meant to move and flow. Like a wave in the ocean, emotion can crest and expand. It can be navigated so that it becomes a meaningful ride. By unravelling my past through the perspective of energy, emotion spoke so deeply to me. It's something we're taught to hide, but should fully embrace. It connects us all as human beings.

You are allowed to move past trauma. You are allowed to move past pain. You are allowed to feel and love your emotional depth. Your sensitivity is a gift. Rather than suppressing who you are and what you've been through, I encourage you to let yourself look at it. Sit with it, see what it has to say. Love yourself for it, and then move it. Move your body, move your breath; use your voice for sound healing. That painful thing is breaking your heart open to change your energy and claim your radiance. The power is always yours.

My legacy is to inspire change in the realm of mental health and wellness. It is to teach and guide all people to embodiment of their truest self from an energetic standpoint. This empowers and aligns you with meaningful moments and situations, it sparks your purest compassion and power. The essence of self-love and personal power through simple tricks and tips make everyday life, (and even the dark night of the soul,) fulfilling and meaningful. This standpoint has aided me through countless avenues. I've allowed myself to fully choose and believe in me. We are all meant to be leaders of our world, and your impact is greater than you even know! By learning about your energy and beginning to find ease and understanding of your magnificence, you can find peace and serenity from inside.

When we are working on the energetic plane, we can heal faster. The phase of an unhealed frequency shifts, and everything around it will shift. By pairing vibrational healing with incremental steps in daily rituals, you'll find yourself in a place that is sustaining a new vibration. Situations will fall into place. Synchronicities will speak to you and your third eye will open. You'll feel rooted and grounded. Vibration makes everlasting change.

This work allows people to know and trust themselves in a fundamental manner. Mindfulness paired with energetic mastery brings people in tune with their soul, which is a calm and powerful place to make decisions from. By discussing current challenges, we can determine where energy might be lacking or where it may be running rampant. Learning is an important part of the game, so that you may be able to access and understand your own unique energy. By combining discussion with knowledge, and energetic healing work with embodied yoga and meditation, much can be uncovered and shifted. Growth is witnessed in numerous ways. For instance, it could be encountering a similar situation that may have been challenging in the past, and being able to choose a different state of mind, response, or action. This makes you more aligned with your values, energy, and power.

Imagine if scientists, politicians, industry leaders, and professionals of any sort were to be fully connected to their feelings, their creativity, and their expression. Imagine if they had a full understanding of their compassion, their motives, and their energy or aligned trust in themselves, so that we can change this world together. In energetic alignment, you are compassionate, caring, and rooted; you are confident, truthful, and serene; you are creative, voice-activated, and listening; you are sure of your purpose. You have love for yourself, your journey, those around you, active causes, and this planet. The energetic self is your greatest teacher! You become the person who is shining authentically, trusting themselves wholeheartedly, and radiating that trust and authenticity into the world.

ABOUT THE AUTHOR

JULIA RUGO

Julia Rugo is an Energy Alignment Coach, Radical Wellness Advocate, and Yoga + Meditation Guide. She believes everyone has the ability to heal and transform themselves from the inside out. She helps teachers, wellness guides, and spiritually-minded professionals understand, clear, and magnetize their internal world for aligned impact across all aspects of their life.

Julia founded her business Julia Rugosa with inspiration from the New England beachfront that she grew up on along with experience from her own journey with mental health, personal power, and spirituality. Her term "radical wellness" encompasses a unique approach to the interdependence of one's physical, mental, emotional, and spiritual health. Julia bridges these elements together for ultimate wellness in her coaching programs. With a formal education in acoustics and frequency engineering, Julia loves to blend science and spirituality for an all-encompassing picture of embodied yoga and empowerment.

Website: www.juliarugosa.com
Instagram: www.instagram.com/juliarugosa/
Facebook: www.facebook.com/julia.rugo/
Facebook Group: Energetic Buds & Blossoms FB Group— www.facebook.com/groups/1275812799439570

17

KATELYN ANNEMARIE BRUSH

FINDING THE MEDICINE

Living a life that inspires a legacy is a science. We've each been put on this earth to figure it out, but there's a catch. Numerous scenarios will test you. Infinite running thoughts will move through your mind. Your journey will either be fueled by those things, or it will feel constricted, slowed down, and even paralyzed by those things. It's truly a puzzle designed for your unique inner knowing to solve. A great deal of the scientific method that will crack the code to your legacy is simply this: not hustling past those things, but transcending them. Creating your legacy is a practice of trusting that everything you need is within you, even when it's scary or your ego seems doubtful.

It's a practice of expansion, but then there's that catch…the tests. The experiences that separate us from fulfilling our legacies are often a soul contract; a lesson that your soul needs to integrate and evolve through during this lifetime.

The truth is, we can either make the hard choices now, pass the test and expand, or the easy choice now, live a hard life and face more tests later. The truth is, also, that there's medicine in all of it, whichever path you choose. It's just a matter of discovering the lesson and finding a way to turn it into your strength.

My experiences led me through one of the biggest lessons I could imagine–death–and because of it, I promised that my life would be one that feels good and honors me. I promised that if I would only be on this earth for a short time, it would be the most liberated and joyful time it could be.

For me, this was my soul contract. I recognized it as my fear of death and my interactions with it. It took me the better half of a decade to really figure out that the lesson I was meant to learn from death was to be brave, trust, lean in, and allow the path of least resistance to give me the right momentum. After years of healing work, the fear of death fueled my desire to live the best life imaginable before the good old reaper comes waddling in to bring me off to wherever land to eat spaghetti with my grandpa...or reincarnate and come back to learn my lessons again, but better? Whatever happens at the end of our lives, my soul contract taught me that I better have one really amazing story to tell. It also taught me that living a memorable life didn't have to be hard, but I could overcome hard things in order to find simplicity in the extraordinary.

We all experience that moment that changes us deeply. Those moments that remind us of life's fragility. The reminder that life is like a pile of powdered sugar; fragile, but sweet. It can change as quickly as the wind picks up. In between the duality of soft and sweet, you might find a range of experiences. Anything from scream crying to laughing so hard your stomach hurts. It's the complexity of life and its inevitable end that remind us how valuable our time is.

Before going further, let's make sure we're on the same page. Healing the fear of death doesn't mean lying down and letting death come. It means healing the fear of anything out of our control such as failure, change, a missed opportunity, and yes, loss.

Growing up, I always threw my shoulders back and said, "I'm not afraid of anything!" The reality was, I was terrified of my future. For years, I didn't believe I'd live to see the age of thirty, and to me that was normal. I was eighteen years old when first diagnosed with melanoma carcinoma. Cancer wasn't the challenge; it was my perspective on life afterward. It was as if that powdered sugar metaphor about life was supposed to say, "Life is like a pile of rotten fruit." I was too afraid to stick my tongue out and taste it.

I tip-toed. Every area of my life became a space I felt the need to move through like I was made of glass. I was careful not to make too much of an impact because deep at the root of my limiting beliefs was this seed saying, "You'll die young." It was so deep that it grew roots, and a big tree of beliefs was formed from that little seed. The branches of that belief system blocked my voice, self-expression, bravery, love, everything….For years it was like living with a tornado looming and nowhere to run. I had no control. Everything was happening *to* me.

That first diagnosis was in May of 2009. I was diagnosed and rushed into surgery. One week later, my grandpa passed peacefully in his bed in the apartment we had built for him in my childhood home. Adulthood kicked me in the face and I felt really unwelcome to take up space as I grew into a woman because I thought it would inevitably end. It always felt like the melanoma would come back, but worse.

The fear manifested into other illnesses. Soon, I was constantly a victim of some inconclusive diagnosis. The panic attacks I had from my teenage years evolved into fainting and years later, the fainting developed into seizures. I had these terrible beliefs that I could never survive in this world, let alone build a legacy worth remembering. Was I destined to forever receive confused, surprised comments from nurses as they read my chart?

Everything felt out of my control until one day a switch flipped and the lights turned on. I felt sweet surrender for the first time, and it just so happened to be in a college yoga class, laying on the cold floor of a dorm building. Eventually that led me to getting my yoga teacher certification, which is where I was introduced to Ayurveda, a 5,000+ year old medical system closely associated with the science of Yoga. Today, I have a flourishing business helping soul-purpose driven leaders launch and scale their online businesses through strategies that align with their unique energetic blueprint. Without all of that struggle, I don't know that I would be here, achieving what I am today and helping entrepreneurs worldwide.

When that happened, I learned something on my yoga mat that changed everything. There are life cycles and a purpose to all things. Eventually through a lot of healing, my tree of beliefs lost its "fear of death" leaves. It started to bloom into thoughts that said, "Yes, that can be true, and you can also live fully while you're here." This was after years of those thoughts sounding entirely different. The healing kept going. Eventually, that tree of beliefs went through so many seasons that all of the ideas moved from dead branches to nourishing thought processes.

We all get to find growth even in the most unusual places. To transcend my fear of death, I continuously faced obstacles with my health that led to the deterioration of my physical and mental wellbeing, until I saw that this fear was also a gift. It allowed me to begin going all-in on my life, my business, and the desires that I had daydreamed about for years. It's how I found the courage to go after what I really wanted, no matter how different it looked from everything and everyone around me. It's the reason I'm writing this chapter from my home office with the Colorado mountains outside of my window. I created this life because I sat so deeply with the medicine that exists inside of difficult experiences.

When I say I 'sat' with the medicine, I mean I genuinely meditated with death in order to learn more about the lifestyle I wanted to create. In the vision, I saw peace, a flexible schedule, travel opportunities, abundance, and the healthiest body possible. In reality, it took years for that to feel even slightly within reach.

There's a golden rule in Ayurveda: *Everything is either medicine or poison.* What if we can distill everything to be that simple? What if, every relationship, food, sound, scent, feeling, activity, and habit are all just acting as medicine or poison? What if any result you wished to create in your life simply depended on identifying the right forms of medicine in your life to achieve it? Or even, what medicine can you extract from a failure or a redirection in life?

Before I could embody my legacy and share the most nourishing parts of my purpose with others, I was living like a leaf in the grand rapids of my external circumstances. Everything happened *to* me, before I realized it was happening *for* me. I couldn't look at the medicine in everything because I was so focused on the poison. As the lesson began to sink in, death being a reminder of the lives we get to build, I was reborn. I went from a person prone to panic attacks that led to seizures, and a depressed cancer survivor, to someone who realized she was destined to do something meaningful with her life.

So I started writing and illustrating a kid's book. The book, *Signing Together,* was published in September of 2014, and it was designed to teach children with disabilities and their families sign language so that they could communicate. I wanted to do good in the world, and I wanted to see the book donate revenue to a nonprofit organization. What I didn't realize in the moment was that this was the first time I really said, "Yes," to building my legacy and leaving a life worth remembering.

The book took off. It was published, reached its financial goals, paid for a designer, and donated to the foundation. Local book shops added it to their shelves. I was featured on radio shows. Things were happening that I had never expected, and then it all took an even wilder turn.

That fall, I was at an open house event promoting the book when the owner of the venue approached me and asked if I did marketing for a living. He hired me, offered to pay me more than I even asked for, referred other marketing clients to me, and encouraged me to incorporate my newly thriving business. This is what I affectionately call "my accidental business baby." I never intended to start a marketing business, but I had always imagined myself living in new places around the world, being a leader, managing staff, and working from my laptop. This seemed like a step in the right direction. I felt more alive doing it.

A year later, in August of 2015, I was feeling lost and less lively. Things just weren't flowing. That old belief system about death crept in. This time it said, "You can't be an entrepreneur, the stress of running a business will kill you." The marketing business was doing well, but I wasn't charging enough. I was tired. I developed a new health issue that eluded diagnosis. I had to pick up a waitressing job and I still felt like I wasn't fully working from home, even though all of my work could be done from my laptop.

That's when I met Randy. I was working at a restaurant on Saratoga Springs's main street during horse racing season. He was in town with a lifelong friend and the two of them were seated in my section. In all my years as a waitress, he was the only patron who ever asked me what I do and what I wanted to do—and *genuinely wanted an answer.* So I told him my story.

"I published a book, and I accidentally started a marketing business but what I really want to do is have an online business with courses, blogs, and products that are earth-conscious and socially-conscious." In truth, I had no idea what I was doing but I knew I wanted to learn how to run a business. Unfortunately, I didn't see myself as someone who would ever be able to, I didn't have mentors or entrepreneurs for parents. I believed it would take me years and cost me a lot of sacrifice in order to learn what I needed. What I didn't know was that all I really needed was a mentor and a nudge in the right direction.

Luckily for me, this man from New Orleans was at my table on the patio. When I finished my story, he responded, "I want to offer you a job" and the next thing I knew, I left the world of waitressing and my little, thriving (but exhausting) business behind to help him build a higher education website. This job was everything I needed, it included working remotely, learning new things, getting better at old things, and gave me a behind the scenes look at a startup while learning from a man who was one of the best leaders I've ever met. Every one of his employees had a story about how Randy had made their lives better, and I did too. He was a business owner who showed me what success and kindness looked like and how powerful it can be when heart-centered leaders build thriving businesses. That was his legacy. It's what sparked my desire to help entrepreneurs find the path to their success because I saw how big the impact could be. It's also what proved to me that it would be possible to achieve both health and wealth.

Fate has a way of pushing us, though. Fast forward to a year and a half later, and I was let go. This man who had come into my life, taught me so much about business and leadership, had to invest in his startup in a new way. At the time, I was in Hilo, Hawaii and on the other side of the phone, I could hear my boss letting tears flow while I looked out onto a jungle in bewilderment of this loss we were both experiencing. He ended up offering to refer marketing clients to me, and next thing I knew I was right back to the universe showing me that it was time to truly trust in my ability to build a successful business.

I could have looked at this in one of two ways: a block in the road, or a catalyst. I chose to see it as the latter. Everything can either be medicine or poison.

It was a full circle moment of, once more, recognizing how easy life could be if only we could see the medicine within our circumstances, no matter how difficult they may be. How many times in our lives are we being pointed in a seemingly new direction? How many times is that actually just bringing us closer home to ourselves?

This was a perfect case of rejection embodying redirection. Many times, we take failure for granted. We as a society see failure as a *poison*, or even a form of death, when really it's a form of *medicine*.

It's an opportunity. In reality, this experience was everything I needed in order to skip a lonely learning curve that could have taken five years. Instead, I learned it all in a year and a half and it didn't take long before I had more clients, raised my rates, and earned more in my business than I made working for the start up. With my marketing business back in action, I also built a thriving private yoga practice. Not too long after that, the path of least resistance showed me the way when I began business coaching. Each scenario that could have been interpreted as bad, was actually something activating more life within me.

The new paradigm of the world we are co-creating together requires us to find medicine in everything. This is where we take our power back.

Each time we learn to nourish ourselves, we are not only redesigning the system we live in, but releasing the tendency to hustle and disconnect from our true nature. We create space for ourselves and others to have success that is simple and feels good. It all starts with saying enough is enough and sucking the venom out of your life so you can truly live.

A lot of the time, your legacy is right under your nose. It's nothing crazy complicated. It doesn't require you to sacrifice your wellbeing, relationships, or values. It doesn't require that you suffer in order to be valued. It may bring pain, but the suffer-fueled struggle is optional. In truth, it asks that you surrender more fully and evolve into the highest expression of your soul's desire.

When you look at your approach to your legacy, answer the following questions for yourself:

1. What is easefully creating results?
2. What's fueling me with joy?
3. What feels like poison (e.g. belief systems) and how can I let go?
4. What opportunities are right under my nose, right now?

When I think of how I want to be remembered, it's a legacy of grace, easefulness, and inspiration. I want to be remembered for the revolution I create by letting my experiences be medicine directing me to success. I don't want to be remembered for pushing on a pull door but being brave enough to go the road less traveled simply because it's the best road for me. The most medicinal and joyful road.

Dear legacy-leading woman,

Look at what is simple, and trust it. Surrender to it.

Together, we are rewriting the codes that were stitched into the fabric of humanity for too many years. We are reclaiming what success looks like. Your very existence is proof that this is your birthright. Let your legacy live through you, and change the world from the inside out.

Rooting for you,

Katelyn

ABOUT THE AUTHOR

KATELYN ANNEMARIE BRUSH

Katelyn Brush is a Soul-Business Strategist. Her mission is to help soul-inspired leaders make more income and impact doing the work they love. She believes that when we rise in success, in community, and into our higher selves, we raise the frequency of the planet. Katelyn's unique approach of infusing the wisdom of Ayurveda into business helps soulpreneurs align and amplify their success for more of a positive impact on the world. Inside her signature program, the Soul-Aligned Business Academy, she guides heart-centered entrepreneurs in building businesses that stand out online and honor their unique genetic blueprint.

Website: www.katelynannemarie.com
Podcast: https://podcasts.apple.com/us/podcast/soul-purpose-driven/id1522519739

18

LÍGIA LEITE

WHY YOU ARE ON A GIANT BALL
FLOATING IN EMPTY SPACE

(and how to crack the code to your lifetime with a Disney movie)

The story asking to flow through me is about remembrance. Because if you are here reading this, you know that there is *something* about to unlock for you. You have been carrying this heat in your heart, asking to take up space. It feels right, exciting, confusing, and quite scary too—because you just *know* that this shy spark can turn into a wildfire. You can't fully see it, but you feel it. And that's where we want to start.

I come from a lineage of shamans, healers, priestesses, wise channels and medicine women in Brazil. My initiations started when I was about five years old, when my grandmother and I would communicate with angels and go down the trunk of a tree together in an altered state for shamanic journeys. We would meet with witches and spirit animals that guided us in the astral realm. I would receive messages in dreams that she would help me read and understand in the morning. I would get to know each Archangel by name, color, and 'personality'. And in waking life, we would have rituals for *everything*—up to this day, if I can't find my keys or that pair of earrings I am sure I still have somewhere, my first response is to talk to Saint Longinus (and promise him to jump three times when he takes me to my lost little treasure. It has never failed me in thirty years.)

Fast forward a couple of decades (and a few years more). After following the breadcrumbs through versions of myself as a camp counselor, Broadway aspirant, translator, teacher, travel journalist, startup manager, event planner, and mindset coach, I am now leading hundreds of women online with my psychic gifts. I am hosting women's circles, pulling cards, seeing into their purpose, speaking my intuition… and second-guessing everything. *'These people are paying me to speak what I am feeling. I am a journalist. I can't fact-check their past life! Goodness, I have become the crazy crystal and incense lady. (Hey, Siri: add 'Get new piece of rose quartz' to my shopping list.) Am I just fooling myself? Who can guarantee that I am really cut out for this?'*

Following what you love and wondering what the catch is (So… I just enjoy myself and make money? That's it?); hearing your parents' daisies-or-lilies dilemma and remembering, out of the blue, that you are different; fake-laughing at the pub with the middle school gang and getting that gut feeling that something snapped that can't be restored; or finding yourself writing John from Accounting for the fourth time that you ordered 9, not 12 new staplers. One way or another, we will all eventually be faced with the question: *but who am I, really?*

That's something I didn't know how to address but couldn't ignore —like a massive piece of spinach on their teeth on an awkward first date. The more I tried to just keep working and doing my thing, the more it felt like I was dragging this heavy pending problem around. The more I tried to *think* myself into really believing in my work and gifts, the more I would question it. No matter how many mornings I wrote down, "I am a successful, powerhouse, intuitive business owner," it would not soothe that craving, that feeling like a part of me was missing. It felt too general. And a little bit like a lie. See, I actually *liked* what I was doing—but I realized I didn't know my voice. I didn't know my purpose. Sure, I knew my job title, label and business tagline by heart, (*I am an intuitive who helps women with X, Y, Z...,*) but those things were what I *did*. They were not *me*.

So I followed those who seemed confident and clear, who I thought never questioned *who* they were, *what* they were here to do and *how* they were here to do it. (Spoiler alert: there is no such state. We are simply in a constant and fun process of fine tuning, coming closer and closer to our essence). I looked for their secret, tried their strategies, and unconsciously started to imitate them in my own work like playing dress up — woo woo boss lady style. I tried showing up in certain ways, talking and dressing in certain ways, launching programs and offers that looked a certain way. It was as awkward as trying to walk in your mom's shoes as a kid: pretty, but most definitely not your size. *There must be something I haven't learned yet. If I am not fully clear, if something feels off, it is because I am not there yet. I'm not ready. I must have skipped a step. What do I need to* do?

So I thought, overthought, tried to figure out, did, and then did some more. And then the holidays came. With them came a wave of exhaustion and confusion like I had never experienced.

It was confusing because I *liked* my work. I was having five-figure lunches, making a living, and setting my own rules. I had been through the process of finding what I really wanted to do and then quitting everything else to go and do it. Why did it feel incomplete?

I was in bed for days and couldn't work for most of the month. I was crying. A *lot*. My partner came home one day to a little ball under the blanket, blasting its favorite childhood band from the 90's and sobbing in fetal position. I welcomed him with a slow motion peace sign coming out of the faceless blanket ball. (We still laugh about that one.) I felt too drained to try to pick myself up and 'realign' with all the energy techniques from the past twenty-five years, so I sat. I sat down, breathed, and took baths. Eventually, I welcomed books and easy movies back in. In truth, trying to push wasn't an option anymore. I was done actively trying to figure it out.

In the midst of all those books and movies, there were two that stand out. I watched Disney's *Moana*, (10 out of 10, if you haven't seen it,) and read a novel by Elizabeth Gilbert. Both for fun, both with no agenda, both part of that wave of relief that took me out of business, quantum teachings and personal development stuff for a breather, and back into simply *being*.

In the movie, Moana feels out of place and unsettled, craving more. (Even as I write this, I am 100% singing the theme song):

I know everybody on this island
Seems so happy on this island
Everything is by design
I know everybody on this island
Has a role on this island
So maybe I can roll with mine

So off she goes, sailing away from her village's rules and autopilot and Into the Unknown (oh God, now we're onto *Frozen*).

Things are not looking up and she starts to doubt herself. She wants to give up. Who is she to even be doing this? Who is she kidding? She didn't go to Hero School. She's just a girl who has only ever dreamed about sailing. Yes, she feels the burning desire to explore the waters in her bones—but has she actually done it before? How can she fact-check and find proof that she really *is* cut out for it?

Moana's story, (without spoiling this wonderful treat for you too much,) is about remembering who she has been all along. But more than that—and here is where things start to get really juicy—her role is bigger than her.She is the daughter of the village chief. She is the granddaughter of a witty, daring old woman who likes to break the mold. She is the descendent of generations and generations of voyagers. Remembering who she is isn't actually about her at all; it is about remembering that she is the combination of a Higher mission and a whole set of skills and traits, intentionally passed down. The call was inside of her all along. Not in a cheesy 'you got it!' way, but because it *is* her very nature. The call, her purpose, *is* who came before her, her grandmother's wits and wisdom, her father's traditionalism that triggered her entire journey, and all these things combined. Her existence is intentional and part of a very specific ancestral line and a group of souls who share a mission. And now we're talking.

In Elizabeth Gilbert's novel, *The Signature of All Things*, a woman, a left-brained American scholar from the 19th century, travels to Tahiti. Her journey is a whole other thing, but here is the part that reactivated something in me: in Tahiti, she learns an ancient war ritual where a kind of shaman called the Pa'ao, a channel for the tribe, would psych men up for battle. The Pa'ao would chant the warrior's entire bloodline to remind him of who he is. The Tahitians knew that a warrior's strength comes from remembering that he is not a man, running to kill another man with an arrow; it comes from remembering that the is part of a larger and intentional mission, and *that* is what makes him more than just 'prepared' or 'worthy' of the battle—but ideal. *Meant* for his battle.

Imagine the adrenaline, the fear, the cold sweat, the need for something to shake you up so hard that you could pull up the last single drop of strength and bravery from your body. And then having a cheerleader priest by your side, screaming: You are the son of Aito, leader of the tribe; You are the grandson of Atutahi, who defeated an entire army alone; You are the great grandson of Manua, fierce fighter and the strongest of the village; You are the great great grandson of Nanua, teacher of the children and loved by all…

So I decided to find my war chant and be my own Pa'ao. Who am I?

I am a clear channel. I love to sing, to lead, to touch other realms, to speak. I am the daughter of fair and compassionate leaders, philanthropists and ambassadors of equality; I am the granddaughter and great granddaughter of wise intuitives, shamans, healers, priestesses and gifted medicine women. Of intelligent minds, elegant presences, sparkers of joy, singers and maestros. I am a holder of sacred wisdom, in the exact way that all these parts of me combined allow me to express it.

And who are you? You are the culmination of where you come from, what you have lived, what you have felt, what you love, and you are the intentions, gifts and mission of your lineage. It all came into being through *your* being. You are the higher intention of something that needs to be delivered to the collective in a very specific way. You are the living embodiment of that intention. You, your voice, your body, your story, what repelled you, what pulled you in. Not the actual circumstances, what people said or did, but what they brought up in you. I've been guided. Just like that fire within has been guiding you.

You are not here by accident or mistake. And I say this with the deepest certainty, quoting the spirit guides that speak through me. You are energy, intentionally incarnated into a body, with the tools and desires that support a higher intention. You are part of a larger group of souls. You are guided above *and* below.

Something that often comes through when I am channeling for my clients is how you wouldn't feel a desire if it wasn't for you. When you actually feel the call, it is the last step of a much larger process. It is the validation that something is already in full resonance with your heart and that you are a vessel for it. For instance, I don't feel a heart desire to be a successful football player. I might see one, think it's cool, but that's it. It doesn't trigger that 'HELL YES'. It doesn't magnetize me. Me, exactly as I am at my most natural and effortless state, am most likely not the best vessel for that frequency; for that specific energy to flow and take up space. Now, show me a powerful woman walking on stage, writing books (look at that!), connecting to higher realms, and reaching millions...and you have my attention.

Let's go back to the 'frequency' and 'vessel' talk. Allow my spirit guides to explain: energy always wants to move and take up space. That's what it naturally does. You are energy; your soul's highest intentions are energy; your desires are energy. Desires want to be experienced, to expand, and it will choose the ideal vessels where it has the space to do so. See it as a desire's natural habitat. From instinct, a desire knows which conditions are favorable and which are not, and it won't set camp where there's no water or the exact foods that it needs. You, my friend, are that habitat. Favorable to your desires; *designed* for your soul's intentions.

And here we are, confused and funny humans, wondering *'but am I really cut out for this?'* while if we weren't, we simply wouldn't *feel* that energetic desire. There simply wouldn't be space for it—and that's just quantum physics and vibrational resonance.

If you are curious about what happened after that sh*tshow of a holiday season of overwhelm, rebirth and reclamation, I can tell you that it redesigned my entire business. It redesigned my wardrobe. It redesigned how I see myself. It was like taking a flashlight and illuminating all parts of me, bringing all the corners that were in the dark back to the surface. It allowed me to operate from wholeness, a kind of wholeness that goes beyond shadow work and self-development at an individual level, and connects me with something larger that I am an intrinsic part of. What was my Why became Our Why. It helped me remember my role, my place in a bigger picture and how I am intentionally designed, (and therefore far more than simply 'ready',) for my desires and wildest vision.

I stopped hosting women's circles and timidly hiding behind tarot cards to deliver the guidance that has always asked to flow through me. I closed a membership, courses and pretty much all my previous streams of income. I gave myself permission to be the me that I now remembered: a channel, intuitive and gifted oracle, with traits so beautifully combined and amplified throughout generations. An 'us'.

Today, I embrace how my ancestors, my most innate gifts, and even the hobbies that I pursued *were* my purpose already. Not what I do, and not my job title, but my presence. I have new courses and a signature program fully centered around channeled guidance and the energy activations. I lead sessions where I make quantum 'adjustments' with light codes and powerful channeled transmissions that are completely guided by spirit. My mind is blown each time. Business is expanding exponentially and I have never felt so powerful and free and the same time. And of course, the doubts and fears come up. *Can I really scale to seven figures now? Reach that many women? Host a massive international live event?* (I'll keep you posted.) The thing is, new desires come up, new doubts come up and none of it makes me or my work less valuable. That is what remembering your larger role does. It's not about your money at the end of the month or what Susan from highschool thinks of your weird posts about other dimensions. It's not about you 'failing' if the goal you set doesn't happen. Doubts are not a threat when you are anchored in your unique, extraordinary value for the collective across generations. It makes all these feelings still valid, but not an indicator of anything else, really, besides the fact that you are human. It stops defining what you deserve or what you are capable of—how we would say in Portuguese, "the hole is way below".

It really is a matter of listening: of recognizing and remembering what is already in you, not an answer to seek outside. If I can leave you one encouragement, it is to declare who you are. Think Game of Thrones's Royal Announcement meets Pa'ao. Not keeping it to yourself, not figuring it out, not coming up with it: *declaring* it. For it is already there. List those parts of yourself and who came before you. What stands out and what was passed down. Announce yourself each morning, out loud. Feel it in your body. Remind yourself of who you are; it is information that can be reawakened in your very DNA.

You already have all the pieces you need because you already *are* all the gifts and resources required to carry out a purpose. Your lineage lives within and through you. You are a larger intention in human form, and your purpose is imprinted in you. *Your* legacy is plural.

ABOUT THE AUTHOR

LÍGIA LEITE

Lígia Leite is a gifted channel and psychic. Intuitive entrepreneurs come to her to become crystal clear on their path and next steps through her channeled guidance. Her mission is to fully activate who you are and what you are here to do.

Her name means 'Clear Voice'. She comes from a long lineage of shamans, psychics, healers and medicine women from Brazil, where she started developing her gifts at the age of five. As a third-time immigrant, she now lives with her *gringo* partner in Belgium where you will find her with some good food, planning a trip, or singing show tunes—maybe all at once.

Website: www.ligialeite.com
Instagram: www.instagram.com/ligia.leite.channel
Email: contact@ligialeite.com

19

MEGAN KRAMER

THE BIRTH OF CREATIONS

L egacy is leaving the gifts of love, expansion, and healing to the future generations.

This time is so important as the legacies we've had passed down from generations prior have been wounded, and it is in this revolutionary time where we feel into those wounds and dive deep into the harmonization of the masculine and feminine energies within us.

The true work begins with you here and now.

So, what is this story? Well, it starts off as one that is not unordinary, you know, the one where the young girl has a great life with everything you can imagine from a white picket fence to a loving family, a great house, and amazing friends. It's a story that many of us can relate to.

I was born and raised on Long Island in New York. Growing up, my external environment was in sync. It was everything I could ask for, but still my soul yearned for more.

What more could I want from the outside looking in?
The ordinary life just wasn't enough for me.

This internal hole I was seeking to mask was a catalyst for my growth. It led me into some of my darkest experiences from drug abuse, to toxic relationships, to people pleasing, to cheating, to manipulation. I was rebellious, and when someone or something attempted to control me, I would instantly be motivated to break free through projected anger. I was good at hiding and great at internalizing my truth. I shone radiant on the outside but was slowly dying within, without anyone knowing my inner pain. I was a master at deception.

My life was in a cycle of repeat, until one day I became exhausted from hiding and masking my truth. I was drained and self-sabotaging my own life for the comfort of others. So, I took my power back by setting an internal boundary. No more living with a mask, no more feeling drained and disconnected. No more using or abusing substances, no more saying yes when the true answer of alignment was no.

Internal boundaries feel difficult to set when we've been conditioned to be a people pleaser. It was uncomfortable to face my demons and past decisions; to own up to my mistakes, apologize for my behavior and forgive myself for the actions I had taken in the past. Change is scary, the fear of the unknown is heavy, but you don't see the divine net of the god within you until you trust your body's wisdom and take the leap.

In a moment of darkness, I knew if I didn't take back the power of my life into my own hands, I would no longer have a life.

These shadows and revelations led me to begin my spiritual journey. I no longer felt prisoner to my past as I began finding clarity in my future. I started to say 'yes' to alignment and 'no' to the victim stories and their box of limitations.

I lifted the cloak of illusion and committed my energy and time to evolving, learning, and discovering.

Like many others, my journey was one of self-discovery from a young age to discover more of who I am and soften into the experiences around me while moving through blockages of fear and deconditioning. Yet it wasn't until I became a mother that my deep healing came full circle and my "why" became clear.

InHER Connection

Since I was a little girl, I always had a deep passion for children. I would play pretend house with dolls, pretend school with students, and eventually my love for children led me into accepting a babysitting job in my teenage years in which I was responsible for three beautiful girls that altered my reality in so many ways. The lessons they brought and the reflections they shared all prepared me for the work I do today. I knew this was a calling when I kept attracting more experiences that pulled me into the nurturing mother archetype.

I knew that, in time, I would be with a man I loved and birth children, but at this point in my life, my dream of being a mother was put on hold to step deeper into my career.

After I finished my degree in psychology and business management, I decided to travel to Bali, Indonesia to make my dream of yoga certification a reality. When returning home, I felt an extreme activation happen within my energetic system. My channel was so potent and the vision of what my life would look like was clear.

When you think you have it all figured out, the universe always comes in to humble you, to say slow down and trust, to feel the true depth of surrender.

One month after returning home, I found out that I was carrying another soul within me and from that day on, my life shifted tremendously. I fell right back into the cycle of the fear, I repressed the emotional blockages down further, and shifted my entire life to meet society's narrative of having a family. I got a 9-5 job while working at a restaurant on the side. This all added up to not only a sixty plus hour work week, but I was not honoring my body, not listening to my womb, and fully disconnected from my soul work.

Four weeks before my due date , I was induced for severe preeclampsia. This reality was so heavy and hard for me to accept. This was not *my* plan. I was supposed to have a fully natural labor with my midwives and no pain. I had to let go of my plan and expectation, and remember that the most important thing was active life for this soul and I.

Fifty-five hours later, I heard the words, "It's a girl,"
and at that moment I knew my soul work just got a whole lot deeper.

Birth is a full body surrender, a powerful force that cannot be tamed or reckoned with. It is the ultimate vital life force energy in using your body as a vessel of magic to be expanded and cracked open from every angle. So much was healed from my birthing experience. I myself was rebirthed. My purpose deepened, my presence was a priority, and my service to the world just grew to include impact on the future.

After three days of being home with her, my body started to give out. I ended up back in the emergency room after a blood pressure reading of 194 over 125. This time, I had to not only surrender but heavily reflect. I kept asking myself why this was happening and after a few hours it came into clarity. That 'aha' moment. The universe was forcing me to rest because I wasn't honoring my newfound experience of motherhood.

I learned the importance of nurturing myself and being supported in this new transition. I was wounded in my masculine energy, and my fire energy, also known as *Pitta* in Ayurveda, was overactive and imbalanced. I had emotional blockages residing within me that were causing unease in my body.

This experience was an invitation by my higher power to reconnect to the parts of myself that were being neglected and repressed.

Through my birth, I learned the depths of what I was teaching: surrender and trust, the power of feminine embodiment, and the importance of energy alignment. How to fully be inside your body while birthing as a woman. How to move through the fear of security and reclaim my depths of support. How to work in alignment with my natural inner cycles. How to nurture and honor my womb and heart with grace and truth. Understanding the magic and depth of the woman's body inspired me to deepen my yoga practice to work with mothers.

Women are the closest thing to source energy that there is. Part of our legacy as women is the creations we birth, whether that be humans, projects, programs, ideas, feelings or anything else for which we are the conduit of bringing into this world.

Women are divine magic. We don't need to learn and become magic—we already are. We hold the vital life force of creating and nurturing life from within. We are the goddess in human form.

inHER wisdom

My past has held two experiences where I was not accepting or ready to be the portal of welcoming a new soul into the earth. My first abortion was when I was twenty-one years old. I sat in a space of betrayal from two people close to my heart at the time. I sat in the unworthiness of not being good enough. I sat in darkness in my parents' bathroom, alone in agony mixed with shame and guilt. This was a time in my life when I had to move through trauma to not only my physical body but my emotional body as well.

After the birth of my daughter, my painful menstruation cycle was healing. I was no longer in pain, and I noticed a shift in my body and menstruation tracking. I think that through the birth of Gemma, the decisions of my past were healed on an energetic level.

The work is never done, the depths of your healing eternally invite you to forever explore and evolve.

In October of 2020, the month of pregnancy and infant loss, I received the news that we had lost our baby at 9 weeks. Heartbroken, defeated, and overwhelmed, I found myself in the space reserved for the darkness of death.

The invisible grieving that comes with the event of a soul transitioning back to light is heavy. I felt that my body had failed this soul who desired to come into earth. The kind of overthinking that came with this loss was less about the pain of what occurred, but really feeling the pain of what could have been.

It is through our darkest days that we become the beacon of light for others who experience one and the same.

Through deep reflection and healing, I came full circle to know this soul just wasn't ready yet. In this realization, my inner teenager was held. Understanding that, in my past, *I* had been the one that just wasn't ready yet. This soul was a direct reflection of the healing I needed to step into the next level of my journey. In accepting that this soul contract was guiding this little soul and I to evolve to another part of our story, I gave myself and that soul open-hearted forgiveness.

This transition was something known as a missed miscarriage. My body wasn't aware that the baby didn't grow properly so my body continued to show symptoms. No heartbeat, just pure heartache. The doctors had advised me to get a D&C procedure. I was distraught, defeated, and torn. My appointment was scheduled four days after I found out. But two days of fully grieving passed, and I was on my knees praying when my body realigned in an organic release. I spoke to my body, my god, and rebuilt my connection to my womb. I broke through the walls that I had created my womb to listen to the inHER wisdom as she guided and held me in this broken space.

I developed an intimate relationship with my body and womb, for us to heal together and release what was no longer meant for the highest good in this moment of life.

This experience was another invitation from life: One to connect me deeper to my womb space; one to heal the trauma that has been passed down from generation to generation; and one to hear the soft powerful voice of the inHER liberation of each experience.

You see, the work is never really done. When we experience trauma and suppressed emotion, a full circle unveils the truth beneath the experience to heal a part of us that craves to be explored. My inner teenager was healing from my past decision rooted in not yet being open to motherhood. I didn't realize that these emotional blockages still remained repressed in my energetic field, and yet there they were, coming up to come out. I was holding repressed guilt and shame, and within this experience, I witnessed a shift in my identity and was able to nourish a part of me that needed to be held and forgiven.

I witnessed my womb open up. I felt the pain from my cycles wash away, I felt the connection with my inHER wisdom grow, and my channel with my sacral chakra become clear and in flow. I sobbed, I screamed, I danced, I laughed. I expressed whatever was arising in the present to move deeper into the wisdom of my womb and heart to grieve, accept, and expand.

When we reflect on what an experience is teaching us instead of why this is happening to us, we give the lessons space to guide us to growth and evolvement.

I had to experience the heartache of choice in admitting I wasn't yet ready. This was a process of mastering my energy and embodying my feminine archetype to move through the notion that I was not worthy of motherhood. I had to sit with myself and my wounded feminine choices that held so much guilt, shame and regret in order to reconnect to my highest truth.

I transformed my pain into purpose.

Today as I write this, March 1st of 2021, the month that honors pregnancy after loss begins and I hold my womb in connection to a newly conceived soul that we've called into creation. I sit here in tears knowing that the connection to this sacred center of the womb has evolved once more. That my purpose just gained a new perspective, one of divine connection between our creative energy and the fertility that we uphold as women. It's in the power of reconnecting to our womb wisdom, understanding HER needs, and appreciating the inHER creation she gifts. Today is another moment of expansion that has reminded me why I came here to do this soul work. This is the true power of surrender.

We are forever evolving and so is our legacy.
Thank you our sacred mother for adding another light working soul to the earth and allowing my body to be the sacred vessel it is birthed through.
My legacy just got bigger.

inHER-Creation

After becoming a mother and knowing that I will be the vessel that more souls come through, I knew I needed to take the initiative to heal the ancestral wounds and patterns to be able to pass down a clean slate of clarity and purpose to my children. By doing this work in the world, we not only heal the past lineages but we heal the future generations to feel safe, free and connected. We leave a legacy of love and support.

It is in my power to share that our past experiences and decisions don't define us now. They don't hold us prisoner unless we let them.

I now teach women to harmonize their feminine and masculine energy to create alignment and balance in their lives. I utilize the practices of Ayurveda, feminine embodiment, and energetic clearing to confidently invite you to create and birth a world you desire. When it comes to nature, all creations are one in the same cycle. When you connect to your cyclical nature, you birth new creations into the world through pleasure and empowerment. It is encoded in my essence to be of service to you in your healing and connection through the heart and womb energetics.

Guiding women to reclaim the natural cycles of life has resulted in them birthing soulful businesses, humans, projects, and ideas into the world. When women thrive in their cyclical nature, they gain access to the codes of creation and learn how to implement the manifestation of their next desires whether that is conceiving a baby, building a business, and launching a new program. Through my work, women open up their sacred womb heart channel, reclaim their identity, and birth the inHER creations that are yearning to light up the world.

The inHER creation within you is ready to be birthed.
The door is open sister, the question is will you walk through?

inHER Legacy

Your story doesn't end just because your body leaves the earth.

What story will you gift the future?

What legacy will you leave behind when you transition to your inHER spirit?

The journey is infinite.

An eternal unfolding rose that continues to softly open with grace and divinity.

We leave the rose wide open in connection, service, grace, and truth.

We leave a legacy for the future to know that the full body f*ck yes is the new revolution, that conscious leadership is the new successful, and that we rise together in collective unity.

We leave a legacy for the remembrance that our outer world is a direct reflection of our inHER essence.

We leave a legacy of support to feel safe in the awakening to life.

We leave a legacy for our journey of life to be celebrated and energetically remembered as love.

We leave a legacy to take back our power and reclaim our throne as the inHER queens we are.

We leave a legacy of devotion to unify, empower, and inspire all that is to come.

We leave a legacy of soulfulness and sacredness for the future generations to be free; free of the chains our ancestors carried; free of the limitations we hold; free of the beliefs that we are not free.

We leave a legacy of integration,

to heal, to move, to feel alive,

to serve, to soften, to fully breathe,

to open, to receive, to LOVE.

We leave a legacy in the NOW.

We leave a legacy for LOVE.

ABOUT THE AUTHOR

MEGAN KRAMAR

Megan Kramer is the founder of Collective Reflections. She is an Energy Alignment Coach, Reiki Practitioner, and Ayurvedic Doula. She lives on Long Island in New York with her baby girl and fiancé. Her mission of devotion is to activate women to reclaim their identity and confidently live their purpose by breaking through limitations. She holds the space to help women connect with their womb and heart wisdom to birth new creations into the world. She is a loving mother who empowers mothers and women through energetic mastery and feminine embodiment.

Website: www.collectivereflections.com
Instagram: www.instagram.com/collectivereflections
Email: allthereflections@gmail.com

20

MELISSA LAMBOUR

BEYOND LABELS: FINDING YOUR PLACE
IN THE WORLD

"I am the wanderer, endlessly searching for my place in the world."

Those are the words I once uttered, and continue to hear from prospective clients.

Since I was a child, cartography and geography have fascinated me. Back then, it was planning road trips; today, it's planning my client's next move. It's only natural that I would return back to the study of maps via Astrogeography as an adult. Astrogeography (AKA Astrocartography) is the astrology of place, which helps you discover the best planetary energies to connect with around the world based on your astrology. So, it makes sense that you may feel strongly drawn or repulsed by certain places. Every place has its unique planetary energies that could affect your mood or personality. My lived experiences with travel, energy healing, Ayurveda and identity struggles have been my guiding light as a Reiki AstroGeo Guide.

As I travel in search of myself, the world becomes my mirror.

Travel brings all my intersections to light. Throughout my life I have struggled with my identity and how I fit into this world. Growing up, I felt I lived within two worlds: American and Guatemalan. As a white-presenting Latina of mixed heritage, my identity is often mistaken or misunderstood. Being in an interfaith/intercultural partnership has allowed me to understand nuances between different religions and cultures. My struggles with sexuality also added a layer of complexity that often was in conflict with my family's beliefs. My struggles were meant to be my life's work. I was meant to guide individuals to heal their deep sense of not belonging, while guiding them towards conscious choices. I want to help people feel worthy, even when the whole world seems to be against them.

I believe in going beyond the labels to find who we truly are behind it all. I work with everyone, first and foremost, at an energetic level. Regardless of gender, sexuality, or race, I believe everyone has the right to manifest their wildest dreams. Astrogeography allows you to connect to energies around the world beyond all labels and societal expectations.

INFLUENCES.

Che Guevara's *The Motorcycle Diaries* was an adventure story I deeply resonated with since it was a story of spiritual transformation. It felt like my own journey of self-discovery. My first solo trip to South America actually passed through some of the stops Guevara made on his famous motorcycle journey, and I was not too far from where he was assassinated in Bolivia. His connection to Cuba touches on my astrological Sun line that also goes through Peru! It's no surprise that his revolutionary spirit called me. A few months after my South American trip, I learned to ride a motorcycle to prepare for my own upcoming adventure.

Traveling is so invigorating because it forces me to engage all my senses. It's also made me realize that the truth always lies within me.

I struggled with my sexual identity and culture, and how I could live my truth. Back in the early 2000s, the only mainstream lesbian show that I had access to was *The L Word*. I had to work through my own internalized homophobia, Catholic guilt and shame that had been instilled in me from a very young age. As a teenager, I desperately sought answers in the Bible, and even considered becoming a nun. In college, I often had moral dilemmas that just could not be answered with sacred text. I didn't have many role models, but the book, *Allah, Liberty and Love: The Courage to Reconcile Faith and Freedom*, by Irshad Manji, a practicing Muslim and openly lesbian woman, helped me accept my sexuality within the confines of religion. I had cut ties with Catholicism in my early college years when I realized I would not be fully accepted. However, before entering into an interracial/intercultural/interfaith marriage, I had to deeply consider the implications and expectations of marrying a Muslim man. Manji's words always stayed with me and strengthened me as I navigated my partner's religion and culture. I luckily became an integral part of his family in no time, and cultural differences blurred as we came to know one another. I'm glad we all saw the humanity in each other, rather than dwelling on the differences.

ASTROMAPPING MY AWAKENING.

For a truly immersive experience, I want to take you through my travel journey, along my most influential planetary lines. I had some wild synchronicities and experiences that now, looking back, were all meant to happen based on the energies at play in that region. The people I encountered and the situations I found myself in were all intended. My favorite planetary energy to work with is Venus, which is all about love, sensuality and relationships. It's the energy I most want on my travels since I have done the inner work to keep me focused on my goals. When diving deeper into my Astrogeography maps (Astromaps), I saw the same Venus line run through NYC, Montreal, and Vietnam, which I've visited, and connected with people from Morocco, Ethiopia, and Iraq, where the line also passes. The Sun line goes through Florida, Cuba, Peru and Iraq, which I've visited or connected with people from there. I've also been affected by the transformative energy of Pluto and Chiron near NYC and Montreal. For my next travels, I'm feeling called to tap into the same, but much stronger Venus/Chiron energy in Europe and Africa across the Canary Islands, Spain, Morocco, Egypt, and Turkey. I have big plans to start my motorcycle adventure in that region.

I believe that my sexual awakening was a necessary prerequisite to my spiritual awakening. I finally embodied my sexuality when I visited Lake Titicaca on the border of Peru and Bolivia, which is coincidentally known as the Earth's Sacral Chakra. It was clear after my first-ever Reiki session that my lower chakras needed the most healing. My struggles with creativity and sexuality were obviously linked to my sacral chakra. Also, understanding my Ayurvedic body type (Dosha) helped me discover the best food and environment to keep my chakras balanced. As a Kapha/Vata dosha, I realized that I thrive in warmer climates since I lack the fiery energy of the Pitta dosha.

My sexual exploration began when I let go of a spiritual community and friends that were not in alignment with my life goals. That phase of my life had to die for the next phase to start. If I stayed at my old spiritual community, I was never going to grow. I was still repressing my sexuality subconsciously because I was trying to live this heteronormative life that I had created for myself. Sexuality is not an easy thing to navigate...it's fluid and messy. The Pluto line that I live by and traveled on tends to cause hardships with partners and friends, which is exactly what happened. There was definitely a rebirth and transformation that occurred, a letting go of our old friend circle to let in new, more aligned people and opportunities. Opening my relationship was the first step. Letting go of the possessiveness of marriage and trusting that we would come back to each other willingly. It was the ultimate test of unconditional love and trust in a partner. The processing we had over the course of a year helped build the foundation of what is our re-imagined relationship. It's the ultimate partnership. My root chakra was immediately healed and my sacral and solar plexus chakras soon followed suit as I built up the courage to explore my sexuality. Acknowledging my sexuality was difficult, but taking action was the hardest. There was so much internalized homophobia and shame I still had to let go. I also questioned my place in the Queer community since biphobia and prejudice toward polyamorous relationships was very common within the LGBTQIA+ community.

My journey into the Queer community started with a random Bi/Lesbian Speed Dating event. That led me down a rabbit hole of other queer spaces that same night. It was a whole new world for me. A few months later in Montreal, I was introduced to a few sex-positive clubs. I later ventured on my own to a similar club in NYC. By this time, I had cut my hair super short to play with my androgyny. That's when I finally felt the male gaze shift away from me. I started sensing a curious female gaze, which I welcomed. It felt so good to express my gender on my own terms, outside of societal norms for a female.

Being in a long-term partnership, I had lost myself to codependence. Solo travel allowed me to reclaim my lost identity and independence. My partner did his first solo trip to Japan in October 2018. Upon returning, he recommended I also do a solo trip. So, I got my frequent flier miles ready and booked a ticket into Cusco, Peru and a ticket out of Santa Cruz, Bolivia. I figured out my three week trip that December, day by day, based on other travelers' recommendations. The trip showed me I was more capable than I gave myself credit for. It was also my moment to show up as my most authentic self. I was surprised that most people were unfazed by my admission of being in an open relationship. I was finally free to be myself, moving from shame to fully accepting my sexual liberation. It felt good to not be tied to the same person or expect all my needs to be met by just one person.

I realized later that this Peru/Bolivia trip resembled a portion of Che Guevara's motorcycle trip as a medical student. His journey and reflections are something I resonate with as I try to be of service rather than a person of great prestige. My travels have opened my eyes to the injustices, inequalities and pollution of the world. I want people to connect to these places with great care and appreciation for the people and the land. If anything, I want them to manifest their heart-led goals with the locals in mind. As a child of immigrants, I care that culture and traditions are honored and preserved for generations to come, but also actively ending and healing intergenerational traumas.

A few months later in Vietnam, I met the most striking genderqueer bar manager from Eastern Europe. To this day, I'm not sure if I want to be them or be with them, but I was proud of myself for complimenting them. They inspired me to hone my craft and consider doing business in Southeast Asia, specifically in hospitality. The Venus line was definitely at work in Vietnam since we stumbled into their bar by chance, and kept visiting until our very last night in Saigon.

Summer 2019 in NYC was buzzing with World Pride, which was the first Pride Parade I ever attended. That whole summer I was grateful for a new friend that helped me tap into my Latin queerness with the utmost confidence. On the Summer Solstice, at a famous lesbian bar, I then met the person that checked all my boxes and then some. She had lived in three other locations with the same Venus line that we met on. She also had Sun energy from her place of birth, which is the exact energy that pushed me to become the best version of myself. The fiery encounter was short-lived, but I'll always cherish spending my first Dyke March with her. I loved that she embraced her creativity as an artist outside her primary profession. She was my mirror and showed me all the areas that needed improvement. Transformative Pluto energy was definitely at play here, but her Sun energy is the flame that continues to keep me on my path. Even though we did not end up together, that night will forever be etched in my memories. She set boundaries that I never experienced before and I respect her for that since I would have let myself be consumed by her.

Soon after, I kept exploring my sexuality in Montreal, where my loving Venus and healing Chiron energy intersected. It was empowering to experiment with my gender expression and go out with other women. The freedom was intoxicating! It was something that was difficult to do at home while living an hour outside NYC. I even considered renting in NYC when I got back home, so dating could be easier. However, the expense and the effort killed that idea. Instead it gave me more of a reason to start a business that I could run from anywhere. I also realized at the end of that summer that I had to stop searching for love outside myself. I needed to divert that attention back to myself and rethink my reasons for travel. What I needed was within me the whole time. There was something I had to heal.

GOING WITHIN. STRUGGLE WITH CREATIVITY.

When I finally got tired of dating apps, late nights, and mindless connections, I walked into a local yoga studio initially for aerial yoga in September 2019. I had practiced yoga on my own up to that point, but it felt good to be in community with other spiritual people. Soon after, I attended women's circles where I met some of the most pivotal people who still inspire me to this day. I attended two retreats that fall that opened me up to the possibility of hosting my own retreats around the world. Walking into this yoga studio changed the trajectory of my life forever. It's where I learned about Reiki, Ayurveda, crystals, and oracle cards. I soon became Reiki-certified and dove into Ayurveda. Finding these tools, along with Kundalini Yoga and journaling, finally set me on my path to healing generational traumas. After one of the classes, I was introduced to the Astrocartography map website. I soon learned how to interpret the maps and began to use them to plan out my life. I am forever grateful for the divine nudges that led me to this yoga studio.

My sacral chakra finally feels healed, allowing me to freely express my creativity and sexuality. One way I express both is through the art of Japanese rope play, Shibari. I stumbled upon Shibari at the NYC Museum of Sex in 2018, and got a nudge from the universe to connect back with the practice in 2020. Shortly after following a few Queer Shibari artists, I signed up for a virtual Shibari conference that was based in Berlin, but served a global Queer community. The conference nurtured my spiritual connection to Shibari.

Another way I tapped into my creative juices was building my own business. I kept searching externally, trying to create some masterpiece, when the true masterpiece was within me just waiting to connect with clients. I had a false notion of what creativity had to be and kept disappointing myself. Once I gave myself the freedom to develop a unique service, I began to step into a creative flow. Being of service has been the most gratifying part of starting my business. Analyzing clients' Astromaps brings out my inner child that loved planning family road trips, but instead I'm helping my clients find top places to manifest their goals and make a difference in the world. My unique method connects their inner energies to the outer energies of the world using their five senses. My holistic approach looks at the energetic being with Reiki, then the mind/body connection with Ayurveda, and finally the global connection with Astrogeography.

LEGACY.

Through my unique Reiki Astrogeography services, I help every individual find their place in the world, beyond the labels and societal expectations. My legacy is to make people feel loved, worthy, and at home, wherever they may reside. I understand the feeling of being disconnected from your community. We find home in the chosen communities that we seek and attract. I'm speaking to the immigrants, refugees, and those that come from a diaspora or have travel restrictions. I wholeheartedly understand their sacrifices since my own family had left the only home they ever knew to start from nothing in America. My soul weeps for those who feel lost or displaced, and those that struggle with their identity—those that wish to connect to the land that they'll never see again. I deeply connect with those that wish to find their place. I'm meant to bring the world together by helping others find their way in a tangible, physical form, or energetically from a distance. Using Astrogeography, I empower those that don't have a place or can't physically be there by tuning into the planetary energies of a particular region or bringing energy back into their now by quickly tuning into the five senses across sight, sound, touch, smell, and taste.

My purpose is to connect with those that feel as if they are lost, unwanted, and endlessly searching. I understand the pain of not being able to go back to your home country. My unique life story has prepared me for this moment to help you feel at peace with where you are. Know that you are never stuck, even if physically you may not be able to travel to certain places. I want to heal that wound you carry of never feeling at home, or feeling like an outsider. Your mind is powerful. I hope you turn to the next page seeing that you have a purpose in where you are now, and the possibility to travel or call in opportunities through the energies of place. I'm here to guide you back home...to yourself.

ABOUT THE AUTHOR

MELISSA LAMBOUR

Melissa Lambour is a Reiki AstroGeo Guide. She helps people at a crossroads find their place in this world using Reiki, Ayurveda, and Astrogeography. Her sessions help people navigate their identity and purpose, while discovering the best places to manifest their goals. Her love for travel and her own identity struggles have guided her work. She strives to serve people from all walks of life, especially LGBTQIA+ and immigrant communities.

She holds a BE/ME in Mechanical/Biomedical Engineering and an MBA in Sustainability Management with twelve years of career experience. She is certified in Quality Engineering, Lean Six Sigma Green Belt, and Permaculture Design. She is also a certified Reiki practitioner while studying to be a yoga instructor. She resides in New Jersey, but you'll often find her enjoying a motorcycle ride around a local windy road or snorkeling off the coast of Southeast Asia.

Website: www.melissalambour.com

Instagram: www.instagram.com/melissalambour
Facebook: www.facebook.com/mlambour
Email: me@melissalambour.com

21

PATRICIA LAMBERT GENT

FREE TO BE

I sat at my desk and heard a clink. I was not sure what it was, until I looked down and picked up a round turquoise stone, and then a smaller gold piece. Another karmic loop was broken. Ten days later, I was released from my job in nursing administration. A release it was, as I had known it would be my last job in a hospital for the last eighteen months.

I had a plan for as long as I could remember. The plan for success was that if I worked hard, I could rest and enjoy life later, after I had achieved a family and a career. Like any Type A high achiever, I always wanted, or maybe needed, to be a step ahead. I have always been a high achiever. I could not understand why anyone would not give 110% to anything and everything they did. I was a loud, tenacious, feisty Irish Italian New Yorker. I lived by the mantra: "If you want something done right you have to do it yourself."

There were jobs I thought I wanted, that I thought would fulfill me. For a time, on some level they did, but it was only on the surface. I didn't know that though. I was so sure that once I achieved my goal, I would be able to relax. Yet that never happened because I believed the long hours were needed to make a difference. I put myself in and out of adrenal fatigue numerous times because back then it was a realistic expectation of the job. Of course, everyone around me worked long and hard; we did it together and it was revered. The stress on our bodies and burnout became the norm. I kept thinking the next job would help me feel better, feel different, be secure.

Instead, I worked the same job two more times. That was not without a specific intention to feel different. I was working like I always did, like I was trying to prove myself to the world. With more confidence in the role, I 'should' have been able live life differently. Yet, I still woke up every morning and dry heaved in the bathroom. I remember thinking to myself one morning that I just need to learn how to manage my anxiety. That was the root of not feeling relaxed, and it ran in the family. Clearly, it was a part of me, and like my curly hair, I had to learn how to keep it at bay.

I started with the obvious. I cut down on the consistent 60+ hour work weeks. I worked with a positive psychology coach and former peer who broke my belief that it was impossible to only work around 40 hours a week when he said he rarely goes above 45. And here I was, struggling to get below 55 hours a week. Overall, it did help me reframe my initial thinking. However, I still did not *feel* different. I was still plagued with needing everything to be perfect and in control before I could allow myself to 'rest'. Then I determined that I needed to include more relaxation in my day.

I committed to doing thirty minutes of yoga with an app for at least five days a week. It was okay, except at the end there was a yoga nidra. For five minutes I lay on the ground, legs apart, and hands open at my sides. The first ninety seconds instructed me to relax each area of my body from my head to my toes. I knew it was ninety seconds because as soon as it was over, I could not sit still. The next three and a half minutes of laying in silence was painful for me. I kept checking the time and my mind raced to see how I could distract myself until the bell went off and I was released from the prison of silence. I was trying to trust the process and stick with the commitment; however, the relaxation was unbearably difficult. It went against everything I was taught and believed. How was this an efficient use of my time? What did I gain from literally doing nothing? I was, essentially, unproductive for five minutes!

Despite the horror of silence, I continued to try doing some guided meditations and completed each 20-day series. I cannot say I was much better with that. I enjoyed the discussion in the beginning, but still struggled with the time dedicated to silence. I distinctly remember getting home late from work, which was the norm. After quickly eating some dinner, I lay down on the bench to listen to the meditation. After it was completed, my husband caught me: "What you did gave you no benefit. I could tell you were not focusing on it, your head was still spinning, planning what else you think you need to do." I was annoyed, but he was correct. I could not wait for it to be done.

Rushing to rest became just another way for me to focus on how I could manage my time to get more rest. These attempts to induce calm became something else to do. A checkbox to complete daily. So, when I was tired and stressed with nothing left to give, I could now say, "Yes, I am taking care of myself and relaxing." I continued to work, like I was waiting for approval, not just from others but from myself. Yet, I still had an inner boredom. On some level I felt I should be doing more, living fuller, yet I had no idea what that would look like. At one point, I thought the next challenge was to be an entrepreneur. It would force me to come out of my own shell and would truly be a growth experience. Yet, I cannot say anything in the nursing field resonated with entrepreneurship, so I continued to be left with my thoughts.

One day, I was going through my personal inbox and found an email from the organization MindBodyGreen. I recall that the article suggested practicing a Rose Meditation. I read the article and then watched the video. It started with a question-and-answer session with Guru Jagat, talking about sound technology with kundalini yoga. This was far from the yoga I was trying to do at home! I loved hearing about the yogic science and how the patterns we have set become integrated into our nervous systems and increase our vibrational frequencies. She spoke so confidently that, by the time she finished speaking and was ready to start some yoga, I had to give it a try. Truth be known, I was not expecting to do any yoga when I started watching this video. There I was, on my bed kicking my legs, doing these weird moves and things I have never done before. Afterward, I felt great and knew I wanted to dive in further.

I started digging deeper, learning and studying everything I could. The teachings, the practices, the offshoots. I felt like I made headway with these meditations more than the others I had tried. I focused on one for 40 days. Some were a mantra that I would learn with the music, others had a hand movement. I enjoyed it and it was easier for me as I felt like I was more 'active' in meditation and had something to focus on. Around the time I finished my first 40 day meditation set, we decided to move. My husband had been dealing with some major health issues that made us start to look at things differently. We had been talking about living differently for a while. A slower pace, connected to nature where I felt most at peace. Things had changed over ten years until the only thing keeping us where we were was my job. I wanted to be closer to my family and where I grew up. It wasn't too long after that I got a job there. We bought a house in record time. The house was perfect for us. Lake view, fire pit, and stone fireplace in a beautiful relaxing environment. The purchase process was smooth. And when I moved in while my husband tied up loose ends before joining me, I had time on my own to dive into my practice.

I did not know anyone so coming home to the practice was ideal. At the same time though, the job had some major red flags. I knew it was not right from the first day. I felt it in every ounce of my being. But everyone was so excited for me to be closer to family, friends, and frankly we loved the area. I knew I should leave, but I did not have any idea what to do. I had done this one thing for so long, and the thought of trusting and listening to myself was a foreign concept. I was miserable but stuck it out. A part of me still thought I could fix anything, and another part just didn't know what else to do. What kept my sanity was meeting others in the yoga community.

This was where I was throwing spaghetti against the wall! Venturing into anything I found interesting and exciting! I did a virtual weekend retreat. I explored astrology, especially natal charts. I had mine read and started to learn more about myself. I signed up for Level 1 kundalini yoga teacher training before going to an in-person class, explored the Akashic records, and purchased a tantric mala.

At the time, I had no idea what the Akashic records were. In that experience, I must say, I felt safe and seen for who I truly was. In a period where I knew so much was not right, I felt like this was all for a reason. Honestly, at face value I did not completely understand what was said. What came through was my gentleness that invites and provides others to be expansive - specifically, that I was not gentle with myself. I was hanging on to societal rules and was not generous with myself. We went on, as I wanted to know my purpose in this pain, this job. What was spoken was for me to learn. I had no idea what...I was just suffering through it day in and day out, waiting for security with my husband's job before I made a move. At the end of the reading, I was curious, so I bought a book and learned to read charts myself.

Still with the need for the external validation, I purchased a tantric mala. Tantric malas are made of beads made in the sacred geometry of a Z-pattern. This energetic flow promotes prosperity and personal growth. Magnifying the impacts of the work you are doing, it is said that once the necklace breaks, you have broken a karmic loop! At this point, I did not know what anything was going to look like. I just knew that when I did these practices that I felt better. I believed in the energetic frequencies that were being built, and the physical reminder of the work I was doing gave me something seen in the unseen. The personalized tantric mala was a fun experience as well. A card was pulled for me and we picked out a stone based upon the conversation and the card. The card that was pulled was, "Share Your Voice", coming out of the cave, persecution, expression. It spoke that we all hold a truth that we long to express, and as we shed the layers of our personality, we discover our soul speaking through us with a clear message. The stone was Amazonite, for empowerment, communication and trust. Truth be known, I was not clear on what I needed to speak up about.

What did become clear was how much subconscious fear was inside of me. I realized how much it controlled me. I was controlling and perfectionistic, and my identity was totally tied to my work. This transformation process was so painful, I started to self-sabotage. I just wanted it to be over. And still, I saw my only way out as being away from the job and starting something new. I had lost my passion; I was not in alignment and not sure where to go or what to do. I just continued to dive into my practice. My mala continued to break as I peeled away the onion around my identity with my work. This work world that I created fed my anxiety when I thought I was managing it, and I saw how I was in my masculine energy, so assertive and decisive that I did not let the creative feminine unfold.

It is said that kundalini yoga makes the subconscious conscious. As this all continued to come up, I noticed one day what was not there anymore. It was my anxiety. I was not dry heaving in the morning. I was not filled with chest pain, and my head was not constantly spinning. I was able to be in a more neutral space. That space now opened me up to be able to receive love as I never did before.

One evening, my husband told me how pretty I looked.

I said, "Thank you."

He almost fell over!

We began to speak how I had never done that before. How I always responded with, Whatever" and brushed it off. Not realizing how that always upset him. I never realized it before, that how I felt about myself was being projected onto him and continuously shut him down.

I woke up on a Sunday morning and texted my friend, ""If I do not lose my job Monday, I'm quitting - with or without another job."

This had been going on for too long, and I had to make my peace with the false sense of security I had associated with staying.

She replied, "5:55, (the time I texted her that morning) that's an angel number!!!"

This angel number emerges when there are significant and major life changes that are necessary in your life that are divinely inspired. It is time to let go of the 'old' that is not serving you and align with your divine truth and soul mission.

When I was released from my job, I felt like a weight was lifted. I was excited to now move forward to a new period in my life. The last time I was in a transition like this, I hurried to get to the next step. I wanted to know what would happen next. That had left me miserable, and probably affected those around me more that I realized. I am now enjoying the space I am in, excited for the future but not allowing my life to revolve around it. I am appreciating what I have and building a new beginning. Now, I am changing myself to change the external environment, not changing everything around me. I can enjoy the experience of being in the present and not attaching to a specific outcome. I am exploring myself in a new space and am able to see how it feels.

Now is the time to create a life in true BALANCE, to change my definition of 'success' and to live my life in alignment with my inner self. It is there that I create alignment with the external world around me. As I am here, building something new with kundalini yoga and the Akasha, I can reflect on what is truly meant. With the final break of the mala, I realized that it and the Akasha spoke the TRUTH that I could not see. I was in this place to learn to TRUST myself, LISTEN to myself and LOVE myself by allowing my feminine side to expand.

Somewhere we get lost and caught up in the 'should'. We negate our own desires as they appear to drift away. That is where we feel, in a very subtle way, that something is missing. That something is usually from early childhood, well before the tar of life sets upon us and our bodies. The beauty of this is, we can get that piece back.

You are still in there. We can reconnect with our true selves which do not have the anxiety, the "not-good-enough", the constant need to do something to the point where you have nothing left to give. That is where I connect with the Akasha and kundalini yoga. They put you in a space where you can reconnect with yourself. Back to a place where we are free to be.

ABOUT THE AUTHOR

PATRICIA LAMBERT GENT

Patricia Lambert Gent is the founder of Resiliency Reframed. Her mission is to create a space to revitalize and reconnect through mind, body and spirit. She helps high achievers prioritize themselves and create a life of balance and alignment. Through coaching, Kundalini yoga, and the Akashic records, she empowers clients to tap into their creativity and create a life in flow. She is a Registered Nurse, holds a Master's in Leadership and Management and is a Lean Sigma Green Belt. She interweaves these practices into realistic goals for her clients to bring about subtle shifts that create lasting change in their lives. She is currently living in New Jersey with her husband, and pug Bailey.

Website: www.resiliencyreframed.com
Instagram: www.instgram.com/resiliencyreframed.com
Facebook: www.facebook.com/patricia.l.gent
Facebook Group:www.facebook.com/groups/BODYful
Email: hello@resiliencyreframed.com

22

RACHEL SIMS

FEARLESS WATERS

F ear.

It can penetrate the deepest recesses of our being, making itself known, making itself visible at the unlikeliest of times.

Scaring us into oblivion, hurling us into shame spirals, bringing us into the dark shadows of our being.

It can be immense, yes.
By why do we fear, fear?
What is there to be afraid of?
Why is it present in this world?

On my journey through life, I've come face-to-face with fear many times. I've met it in the jungles of Southeast Asia, the seas of Western Australia, the outer reaches of the universe, and the inner workings of my mind.

But what have I learned?

Fear doesn't have to grip us. In fact, we can utilize it for our benefit. To help empower us, to help us reach greater heights in our life, and to move forward with the shadows as partners—an unlikely duo walking into a glorious sunset.

I didn't understand this for most of my life, but at the same time, I didn't even realize how much fear lay under the surface until recently.

The thrill-seeking adrenaline junkie in me had jumped from planes, plunged off cliffs, swam with whale sharks, and trekked around the world with a map in hand and little else. Taking these leaps of faith without a second thought or worry of the consequences, I trusted myself and trusted something greater.

But as I progressed along my spiritual journey and opened to the depth of my being, I recognized how much I'd been skimming the surface of my existence. Too worried about what lay beneath to approach it and at the same time, totally unaware of what was even down there.

I was fearless on the surface, but beneath it, fear was swimming through every cell of my being.

It was showing up in the way I undervalued myself, in the way I worried about what others thought of me, in the anger and rejection I felt from past partners, and from this immense feeling of lack—a lack I could never pinpoint.

The fear was real.

As I moved forward in my journey, I awakened to something that would change my life forever. Something that would change my perspective on the world, that would enable me to uncover my hidden shadows, open me to a whole new world of existence, and help dispel my great notions of fear.

I had awakened to the Spirit of the Water.

DIVINE CONNECTION

In June of 2019, I felt a calling.

It was a powerful full moon and, after years of strengthening my intuition, I felt the universe and my inner voice simultaneously urging me to perform an impromptu ceremony—one that would involve my Womb Blood and a lake near my house.

The womb is known as a divine center of creation, and I knew it was going to be a powerful ritual. I had previously done Womb Blood ceremonies, but with the earth, never with the water. I had cultivated a relationship with a beautiful tree in my yard, one I had nicknamed the Ancestor Tree, as I had done many ceremonies there —greeting my ancestors, healing our generational lineage, and praying for deep healing for the collective. I wondered why I was being pulled to the water instead of this tree.

But I followed this guidance, and for three days went to this spot to pour out a little bit of blood in various places around the lake, praying to my higher self and guides, and sending out my wishes to the universe.

Within 24 hours, the things I had asked for were being birthed into existence. I had asked for community, abundance, and to help balance my divine feminine and divine masculine energies. In that short period of time, I'd connected with a beautiful heart-centered water community, found a new way to bring in abundance that was in alignment with my holistic work, and joined a course that helped me heal the sexual traumas that had kept my divine feminine and divine masculine in disharmony.

I knew there was something here.

I found I was being guided to water sites, water videos, and water on social media. It was showing up everywhere in my healing work. I started to recognize how little I really knew about water and how much this powerful element was showing up in every aspect of my life.

The more I opened to the water, the more She spoke to me.

I was communicating with Her at the rivers and lakes near my home. I was connecting more deeply with the water I was drinking from the local springs and the Kangen water in my home.

With my third eye developed and my consciousness open, I even began seeing the Spirit in my room, in the in-between state between sleep and awareness—an androgynous being, confident in stature, blue in color, and powerful in spirit. She would speak to me, delivering messages that I sometimes couldn't understand and messages that would make perfect sense, coming to life and manifesting in the 3D world.

I began to understand Her perception of the world and it opened me completely. She helped me see the universe through a new lens and helped to connect me to other Sacred Water Keepers who showed me new ways of existence.

My world was *expanding*, and I was healing more deeply than ever.

As I continued on my journey with the Water, I started to realize how much the Water Spirit had already been with me in my life - in some of the most potent experiences of my past. I backtracked through my spiritual experiences and my travels around the world, and at almost every significant moment of progress, what kept appearing?

Water.

She had been guiding me for much longer than I was even aware.

I started in the Holistic Healing profession as a colon hydrotherapist. A healing therapy that involves – WATER.

I moved on to energy work and moon circles. The moon symbolizes the subconscious, and the subconscious represents deep – WATER!

I then went on to do sexual trauma healing and empowered womb work, which symbolizes and is the center of our sacred—you guessed it — WATERS!

She had been with me at the start of my spiritual journey five years ago, where in the jungled forests of New Zealand I connected with a powerful healing spring called the Riwaka Resurgence. I had journeyed there alone and come face-to-face with a mighty Water Spirit. I look back now and understand my initiation to the Water Path to have begun in this place.

Three sips from this sacred spring helped to awaken something within me and start to remember who I truly am.

DEEPER CONNECTION

With this newfound connection and awakening to a deeper way of understanding the world, I had much come to the surface. Many things that were very difficult for me to face, that pained me at the core of my being, and absolutely ripped at my heartstrings.

The details aren't important at the moment.

What is important is that the water started connecting everything together.

All the symptoms I had experienced after fifteen years of being chronically ill, my distrust, anxiety, and anger in past relationships, and my inability to feel completely whole in my inner and outer world all started to piece together.

I started calling the Spirit of the Water "The Great Connecter", because that's exactly what She began to do.

She was connecting me to those who could assist on my journey. She was connecting me to plant medicine that could help me go deeper. She was connecting me to a community that understood my way of being. She was connecting me to the hidden traumas that I never even knew existed. She was connecting me to the selves and energies that were afraid to be seen. She was connecting me to other realms and layers of existence.

She had become the bridge for everything I couldn't understand, and everything I was seeking.

And best of all?

She helped me connect to fear, and the fearlessness that walked beside it.

She has helped me see that fear is here to teach us. It's here to help us grow. It's here to bring us our greatest revelations and deepest understandings about our true nature.

We've been conditioned to hide from fear, to run away from it, even to hate it.

Yet the Spirit of the Water proves time and again that fear is one of our greatest assets.

FEAR AND WATER

I remember being little and having recurring dreams about dark, black water. Of waves rising a hundred feet in the air, ready to crash down on me in a vulnerable state of panic. I'd wake up in a full sweat, gasping for breath, dazed and chilled to the bone.

I look back and recognize how telling this was for the relationship I'd develop with Her later in life. How my fear of water at an early age prevented me from diving deeper into myself at a time when I wouldn't have been ready. That these dreams were necessary to keep me in ignorant bliss until the time was right for me to face the demons that lay beneath the surface of my subconscious mind.

Being older, a bit wiser, and a lot more understanding, I had the will and the courage to encounter the fear head on.

The Water tested me in an Ayahuasca ceremony. In a place where I met the devil himself, water was my savior. She taught me to reach for Her, to drink Her with love, and to recognize the safety within.

She's tested me in a midnight cold water plunge when it was pitch black outside. In a lake surrounded by ice, She taught me to trust in myself and to strengthen my mind.

She's tested me in the farthest reaches of my heart – with a grand gesture of love, and a grand gesture of denial, She taught me to love myself deeper.

She's tested me in my subconscious mind. By awakening the many traumas and selves that lay beneath, and by unearthing the limitations of my mind, She taught me to remain unattached to identity and life's illusions and see the multi-dimensionality of Self.

Fear was present through it all.

But the more I see fear as an ally, the more I learn to embrace It, to see It as a brother, to welcome It, and to move forward as partners – the more exponentially and exceptionally I have grown.

BALANCE AND FLOW IN ALL THINGS

Fearlessness.

It's been one of the beautiful gifts the Spirit of the Water has taught me. Does it mean I walk through life careless, carefree – as if I'm made of metal and fire, impervious to the wounds of the world?

No.

Fear still creeps in. I still get startled, worried, and unsteady on my feet from time to time. But I'm understanding fear. I'm learning to walk beside it.

The Water Spirit teaches us that everything is in flow. Everything is in constant motion, in constant fluctuation, in constant progress, in constant balance. Life never stops, and nothing is ever permanent— even if our mind thinks it is.

There is such freedom in this idea as it helps us understand that we're never stuck. We're never held back. We're never locked in.

Everything continues on and a greater universal pull helps us move forward.

The Spirit teaches us that there is balance in all things – in the divine masculine and divine feminine, in "good" and "evil", in the ebbs and flows, in the conscious and subconscious. And along with the laughter and joy that exist in this world, they must then be balanced by space for fear.

Fear helps to illuminate the darkness and bring light to our world. We wouldn't understand what light was without it, what would we compare it to?

She teaches us that we encompass all things, that we are multidimensional beings spanning realities and planes of existence, that we embody many selves, many personalities, many archetypes.

With these teachings, how could we live in fear?

Fear stems from an idea that control is lost, and the underlying idea that we even have to be in control. We are such vast creatures with so many layers, we will never fully grasp the entirety of our existence. And with that, we can never be fully in control.

When we move past trying to understand everything, trying to plan every step of the way, and trying to grasp life with a firm grip, we move into a place of peace, trust, and unending bliss.

This is the beauty, the wonder, and the freedom this Spirit brings us.

THE WATER LENS

As I move forward on my journey, I've learned to view the world through the lens of water.

The Spirit has taught me to be more present. Living in the past or the future takes away from the journey.

The Water Spirit has taught me that the present is where we find the most abundance. The precious jewels. The potency.

The love.

This elixir of presence enables us to enjoy the process and the unfolding as we take each step along the path of life, focusing on each moment as it drifts by.

Presence helps me recognize the fleeting, constant motion of life, and how much I want each moment to count. I don't want to remain in the unconscious waters and lead a life of automated responses. I want to be conscious, aware, and responsible for everything I encounter.

For in those spaces are where the growth occurs, where the beauty is recognized, and where the fear evaporates.

The Spirit of the Water has taught me to see life in all its beauty. To see each ebb and flow as an absolute blessing and nothing to be fearful of as they help deepen the human and spiritual experience here on earth.

I've learned to embrace each moment as it comes and remain in that present state, instead of retreating to the dark, unconscious waters when I don't feel like fully seeing what's in front of me and allow the shadows to take hold.

This water lens has shifted it all.

Water is in constant motion, moving with Her energy, moving with Her current. She never apologizes for her ebbs and flows, but fully owns it all. She lashes out with the currents of rage, best recognized as the seas of change in the midst of a summer storm. She rocks the fish to sleep with the currents of peace, seen in the serene trickle of water through a forest stream.

And with each season, each shift in her waters, we are mesmerized. Understanding. And deeply touched by her many forms.

And as we are water, so too shall we move in all our peace and fury. Moving from one self to the next, embodying each energy as it swims by. The more I give myself the freedom to move my inner waters in this way, the more fearless I become.

I envision a day where we can all move in this way. Where we all develop a closer relation to the Spirit of the Water, so we may move in free motion and understand at the deepest level how connected we truly are.

For when we move freely, it ripples out. It energetically affects all those we encounter, allowing the next person to move freely and ripple out to the next, and the next, and the next. Creating a whirlpool, a tidal wave of free movers, thinkers, and shakers.

Highlighting the true connection all life shares.

It may take time for each person to allow their inner waters to move, to break free from their own chains of fear, but once they're touched by the ripples of freedom, it's impossible to shake.

GRATITUDE FOR THE WATER SPIRIT

My life has forever changed from connecting with this great Spirit.

The continuous lessons I've been taught, the enjoyment for life I've recovered, the freedom in being I've received.

The most beautiful thing I've recognized is that this Spirit is so incredible and so heart-opening because this Spirit is me—at the deepest part of my being.

There is no separation.

She is me, and I am Her.

And by allowing this Spirit in, I've allowed my Self in.

I've allowed her to take up space and residence in this world. To be seen. To be heard. To be here.

She has awakened me to myself and the core of my Spirit. She's allowed my inner mermaid to swim freely.

And...

She's allowed the gripping hand of fear, that used to taunt the undercurrents of my existence, to slowly unravel – to disperse and intertwine into the abundant, flowing waters of life that gently guide my vessel home.

What greater gift could I receive in this world than to look the Water Spirit directly in the eyes and witness myself?

To hold Her hands with unconditional love and compassion and say from the depths of my being, "Thank you. Thank you, great Spirit, for welcoming me back home."

For I am.
I am home.
And I am
fearless.

ABOUT THE AUTHOR

RACHEL SIMS

Rachel Sims is a Sacred Embodiment Coach, Sexual Empowerment Guide, and Sacred Water Keeper - but as the waves are always moving and the wind is always shifting, that could change along her sacred path of life. Her mission is to teach the collective about the energy of flow. Life is a continuous cycle of movement across new experiences, shifting mindsets, and unexplored territories. Flow is the underlying current that keeps us in our most present, aligned, and empowered state. In her short 31 years, she has lived many lives, been many different people, and seen many different things. Carrying this energy and mindset and allowing herself to open to the greater energies of the universe has helped her heal from chronic illness, open herself to new opportunities, and gain a deeper understanding of the multidimensional self. These teachings, these learnings are the Legacy she wishes to leave.

Website: www.RachelSimsHealing.com
Instagram: @RachelSimsHealing

Facebook: www.facebook.com/TransflowingLight
Email: RachelSimsEnergy@gmail.com

23

STEFANI SILVERMAN

DESIGN THE LIFE YOU DESERVE

"It is by going down into the abyss that we recover the treasures of life. Where you stumble, there lies your treasure. Opportunities to find deeper powers within ourselves come when life seems most challenging."

- Joseph Campbell

At sixteen years old, my world as I knew it felt as though it was crumbling around me. Everything was caving in—it felt like I was suffocating. I had experienced a bit of anxiety at a young age but what started in 2008 changed my life forever to shape who I am today. Although they were some of the hardest years of my life, when I look back I wouldn't change a thing. I found myself and my true purpose, and my mission is to help others do the same.

Growing up, my father was a high-powered construction project manager in New York and New Jersey. Being the creative I was, it was ingrained in me that I would grow up to become an architect. My favorite days were when he brought me to work, walking construction sites, watching design presentations, selecting finishes and fixtures, and meeting clients with my hard hat and work boots on. I had always felt a greater presence beyond my physical sight within every space. My father was everything to me, I looked up to him more than anyone in my life and he was always so proud that I would one day follow in his footsteps. My father was my biggest cheerleader, encouraging me to always do better and be my absolute best at anything I would do.

Prior to 2008, I was spoiled—and entitled—coming from a household of wealth and always getting my way. Being young, I didn't know any better. I was very fortunate to not have dealt with many "real-life" issues aside from what I was going to wear each day, who was dating who, and managing my good grades in school.

It was a warm, early spring evening on March 3, 2008 when everything I had known to be in my life crumbled in what feels like the blink of an eye. That night was the root of years' worth of abuse, trauma, and heartache like I had never known existed. My father was caught having an affair, and my mother was kicking him out. I was a junior in high school, I had a boyfriend, internships and art classes in the city. I was playing club and varsity soccer. Everything on the outside appeared normal and great. I ensured I maintained the facade that there was nothing wrong, however, my life was slowly spiraling out of control. My parents' divorce was anything but civil. My father, an addict prior to my birth with a list of mental health issues, went off the deep end and we lost everything. That night, I lost the father I knew and loved for sixteen years.

Sports and art became my escape from the new reality I was forced to live every day. I started experiencing anxiety and panic attacks for the first time in my life, and was diagnosed with a panic disorder in 2009. Immediately, my mother placed my younger sister and I into therapy through YWCA, *"a nonprofit organization dedicated to eliminating racism, empowering women, and promoting peace, justice, freedom, and dignity for all. It is one of the oldest and largest multicultural organizations promoting solutions to enhance the lives of women, girls and families."* This therapy was free and saved my life. To this day, I still see that same therapist, and I will never be able to repay her for what she has done for me.

During that time, I had thrown myself deep into playing soccer and building my art portfolio to apply to college. Although I didn't realize it at the time, these distractions were profoundly healing and kept me out of any trouble. Despite it all, I maintained the determination to fulfill my dream of becoming an architect.

Shortly after graduating highschool, I left to spend a month in Greece alone with my grandparents before starting at the Pratt Institute in Brooklyn, New York that fall. I had the summer of my life, spending quality time with family, voraciously reading, meditating on the beach, and running every night in the sunset to clear my head. Coming back in August, I felt like a brand new person. I broke up with my toxic boyfriend, moved to Brooklyn for college, and began one of the most demanding undergraduate programs in the country. Although I had nothing but my mother's $100 a week allowance backing me, she was adamant I graduate at any cost and I still thank her for that every day. If not for her strength, tenacity, and the way she handled herself through the divorce, I don't know that I would have been able to fulfill my dreams.

My father made my time at Pratt anything but easy. As if the program wasn't tough enough, his addictions resurfaced, and I became the receiving end of every phone call. For those unfamiliar with architecture school, there are approximately one hundred and sixty eight hours in a week, with one hundred and thirty of them spent in class or in the studio creating, researching, and building complex architecture projects that will be critiqued by professionals at the end of each term. Regardless of what you're going through outside the program, it is by no means an easy feat. For years, it felt like I was swimming upstream, exhausted and gasping for more air. I was introduced to the practice of yoga, journaling and meditation, which had all become crucial to my survival and had a profound impact on my ability to continue through the program.

THE LIGHT

It was during my undergraduate thesis term at Pratt Institute that I found and fell in love with *feng shui* and the psychology of architecture and design. I had been building and designing a shelter for women and children affected by domestic violence which focused on promoting safety, comfort, and healing. Through my research, I became obsessed with the principles of feng shui—how our environments can support or hinder everything about the way we feel and how and what we manifest.

I started slowly implementing my findings within my own space, an eight-foot by thirteen-foot room within a small, four bedroom, five hundred square foot apartment. It was then that I started to *feel* different. My anxiety and panic started to slowly dissipate, I was sleeping better, and my friendships became enhanced. I traveled to Israel, Puerto Rico, and Greece, and landed my dream job in Manhattan with the salary I asked for. It felt as though I had finally cracked the code. Our environments have a direct relationship to our inner state, and feeling good, supported, comfortable, and safe within my space made me thrive as the best version of myself.I had the strength and support within myself to become my own cheerleader, not relying on my father or anyone else backing me like when I was a child.

After graduating with my Masters, I went on to study and obtain my certification in feng shui. My goal was and still is to bring these principles to the masses and teach others how they can change their lives. By combining my technical design background of architecture with feng shui as a healing tool, I've been able to piece together my clients' lives and make adjustments for significant improvement. Together we work to investigate where the blockages lie in your homes that are holding you back from having what you truly desire. Using the power of feng shui, we remove these obstacles in order to attract new opportunities and good fortune, creating a better flow of energy in your home that will in turn create a better flow in your life.

CHANGE YOUR SPACE + CHANGE YOUR LIFE

When starting with feng shui, you'll soon realize the vastness of possibility you have to change your life by changing your home. My advice is this: take small steps.

Feng means wind, and *shui* means water. Not coincidentally, these elements are associated with health and wellbeing. Feng shui, then, is the use of wind and water elements to promote health and well-being. The primary principle surrounding feng shui beliefs is that everything—including you and me, your pets, your furniture, the colors in the space—gives off and receives energy. This energy is called *chi*. There is a constant transaction of energy between objects and living organisms.

When you open your mind to the possibility that everything is energy, then you are well on your way to shaping your universe. When you begin to purposely and intentionally focus your thoughts on what you want, then you literally begin shaping your future reality.

Along with the internal, your external environment can be a powerful tool for manifesting success, abundance, happiness, love, joy, passion and anything else you wish for. Feng shui has opened my eyes and mind to the impact that the environment can have on one's life and health. It opened the doors for me, and has become the foundation for the way I've built my company--committed to helping and teaching you how to create an environment that feels good the moment you step through the door. You can exhale, your mind and body relax, and a peaceful feeling rises up. You are in a space whose sole purpose is to support you, your needs, goals and dreams. Everything is in alignment, and is designed to improve your health, prosperity, relationships and overall happiness.

I have always felt a greater presence beyond my physical sight within every space. All my life, I intuitively tuned into it and used it for a source of good. I refer to it interchangeably as vibes, energy, vibrations, and other terms too. What we call it is irrelevant.

Connecting to it is imperative. Realizing this connection and implementing the ancient principles of feng shui have directed the course of my life. Tuning into it has helped me heal PTSD, undo fearful beliefs, and live with clear purpose. By enhancing the space around me, I am able to co-create the world I want by aligning with good-feeling emotions and directing them toward my desires. I create spaces that support and guide the ability to tap into an unlimited source of creative energy, wisdom, and abundance.

As I grew, and as my life and intentions began to shift, I was able to make adjustments within my space to better support my needs. It began with baby steps, first creating a space with the intention to make me *feel* better. Giving my mind, body, and soul the space and continued support I needed to heal from my past grief, trauma, and anxiety. I then was able to focus on shifting the intention to my career, then love, health, relationships, etc. That is what I love most about feng shui. It is not a "one-stop-shop", and there is no one "quick-fix." The goal is always a well balanced home in its entirety, but as we grow within a space and as life happens, feng shui also grows and shifts with us. In the last 10 years, by implementing the principles of feng shui I have been able to attract the love of my life, work my way up to a management position in my career, more than tripled my starting salary, and graduated a masters program. I've been able to better manage my anxiety, attract the people who provide the support for me to heal, and better my relationships with family and friends.

That is how I arrived to the point I'm at today, and my goal is for you to also do the same.

FENG SHUI FOR BEGINNERS

I am able to see clearly how my struggles have been part of a bigger plan to help me strengthen my faith and trust in the world around me. I've chosen to perceive hard life experiences as opportunities for growth and healing, because nothing happens by accident. It has led me to explore the deeper meaning of everything around me, and to not settle at surface value. Now I am honored to help clients achieve great, life-changing success by manipulating the spaces within their homes.

When you are living in alignment with your space and your environment around you, you will no longer feel blocked by fear or negativity. When implementing the principles of feng shui, you must be willing and committed to change the way you think, act, and live.

Once you claim your power and design the space you deserve, the question becomes: *What will you do with it?* When you feel good, you give off a presence of joy that can elevate everyone around you. Implementing the principles will empower you to live your life purpose, and they will amplify abundance, happiness, health, and peace. By the time I close a project with clients, they not only feel change within their home, but they have a greater understanding of their higher purpose as well.

To successfully create the life of your dreams, you need to first familiarize yourself with some feng shui basics. I recommend working with a professional to achieve the most benefit beyond the few I've outlined below to get you started

FIVE ELEMENTS

In feng shui, we use the five element system from Taoist philosophy. This system looks at the cycles of nature and how they work together to be in balance. The five elements are earth, metal, water, wood, and fire. Each element is associated with certain qualities, as well as colors and shapes that can be used as design elements if you'd like to enhance those qualities in your home and life.

Earth

Earth is related to self-care, boundaries, and nourishment. It's connected to earthy colors like yellow, orange, and brown, as well as square shapes and heavy objects. You can add the earth element to your home with a square yellow rug, or a solid rectangular desk.

Metal

Metal has the qualities of joy, beauty, and precision. White, gray, and metallic colors, as well as circular shapes, represent metal. To add metal to your space, try adding a round, metallic planter or light fixture.

Water

Water represents deep wisdom, as well as our connection to others and the world around us. It's connected to black, very dark blue, and wavy shapes. You can add water to your home with a water fountain or artwork with watery images.

Wood

Wood is related to growth, healing, and vitality. It is represented by green, blue, and teal, as well as tall, columnar shapes. Green houseplants are an especially great way to introduce the wood element to your home.

Fire

Fire represents passion, inspiration, and visibility. It is related to fiery colors like red and bright orange, and triangle shapes. Light is also connected to the fire element. Lamps are a great way to add the fire element to your home.

COMMANDING POSITION

The commanding position is one of the fundamental basics in feng shui. It is important that your bed, desk, and stove are all in command, since each of these items represents a significant aspect of your life. Your bed represents you, your stove represents your wealth and resources, and your desk represents your career and path in life. In order to place your bed, desk, or stove in command, find a location in the room, so that when you're sitting at your desk, lying in bed, or cooking, you can see the door without being directly in line with it. The idea behind this position is that you have a good view of anyone or anything that could be coming in through the door, which helps you feel more at ease on a subconscious level. It also means that you are more aware of potential opportunities that might be coming towards you.

THE BAGUA MAP

Working with the Bagua Map is one of the most powerful ways to create positive changes in your life and is essential when incorporating the principles of feng shui. The Bagua Map is a nine square grid that you will lay on top of the floor plan of your home or office. The front door will be at one of three guas, or sections. Wisdom/Knowledge Gua, Career Gua, or Helpful People/ Travel Gua.

Once you lay the Bagua Map, you have a clear indication of which areas of your home correlate to different areas of your life. Take notice of these areas and rooms, and how you feel. Are they cluttered? Does they need some T.L.C.? When you think about these answers, it will begin to illuminate for you how you're feeling and the thoughts around these areas.

For example: if your wealth area is cluttered and messy, you may often feel like you don't have a handle on your finances.

The good news is, if you don't like the story an area or areas of your home tells, you can change the story.

DECLUTTER

When you clean and declutter you not only increase the positive flow of energy, you also make room for happiness to come into your life. Clutter has a profound impact on your emotional, mental, physical, and spiritual well-being. A healthy home has healthy energy and healthy energy is moving energy.

Now that you understand the areas of the Bagua Map and how the areas may impact your life, as you're cleaning, it is important to understand what you're cleaning out--physically and metaphorically.

Clean with intention. Understanding which area you are in, and what will improve when you clean. Decluttering goes beyond organizing your things. You can also clean and declutter mentally and emotionally, your schedule and what you feed your mind.

FINAL THOUGHTS

Creating a better flow of energy in your home will create a better flow in your life. I am committed to helping and teaching you how to create an environment that feels good the moment you step through the door. You can exhale, your mind and body relax, and a peaceful feeling rises up. You are in a space that's sole purpose is to support you, your needs, goals and dreams. Everything is in alignment, and is designed to improve your health, prosperity, relationships and overall happiness.

I invite you to take advantage of the powerful transformation that we can help you achieve in your spaces.

ABOUT THE AUTHOR

STEFANI SILVERMAN

Stefani Silverman is an interdisciplinary designer experienced in Architectural and Interior Design. A Feng Shui Expert certified by the American Feng Shui Institute, and a Reiki Practitioner, she can infuse Reiki into everything she creates. Stefani is committed to guiding and teaching individuals to rewrite their story and design the life they deserve.

Her company, Iasis Design Lab, a full-service interior design, and Holistic Feng Shui company, as well as her blog, grew from a place of deep trauma. Through all the darkness, Stefani was able to find her calling to heal herself and others through aligned and supported spaces.

After more than a decade of experience and study, through 1:1 clients and transformational group coaching and courses, Stefani has successfully guided and designed sacred, peaceful, and supportive spaces for several clients. Everything is in alignment, and is designed to improve health, prosperity, relationships, and overall happiness.

Websites: www.stefanisamantha.com
www.Iasisdesignlab.com
Instagram: stefanisamantha

24

STEPHANIE HEATH

HOW TO BECOME A REALLY RICH RECOVERED PEOPLE PLEASER THROUGH SOULWORK

EMBRACING YOUR *ISH:

I was a terrified empty shell, a people-pleasing chameleon.

I hated myself but didn't know it. My amazing, beat all the odds, Jamaican born parents loved us...but like many immigrants spent a lot of time working. Society wasn't a good replacement. It rarely positively reinforced self love in little dark skinned Black children; especially girls. So, safe to say, I didn't have many internally driven reasons to accept myself.

And so, I decided to turn into the accomplice. I was the bestie to the pretty girl in school, at work and in university. I saddled up to them, hid behind them, and danced for my scraps.

I was the low-key annoying friend, the one you **always** had to affirm with:

"You're pretty."
"You're worth it."
"We like you; stop worrying."

I had different sets of friends for every season. I had my church friends, where I was "church Steph," my dance club friends where I was "dance Steph," my Martin Van Buren friends where I was a "unique dresser but still annoying Steph," and my Long Island City friends where I was "new girl Steph."

I remember one day in high school standing on the subway platform, waiting for the train and thinking, "Who am I?" I honestly didn't know. I think at the time, (maybe you can relate) I didn't know how or where to learn who the real me was. I didn't even know where to start.

My first job was with a group of tight knit, hardworking recruiters at an agency in the Financial District of Lower Manhattan. Only Lord knows how I got that role. I suppose when you grow up in the lower middle class, you're still hungry enough to choose a large commission-based salary over the safe HR Assistant role I was also offered at the time.

One of my colleagues in particular stood out. Being around her, I learned so much about taking responsibility, real confidence, and how to get it.

She taught me that you become confident by accomplishing things and owning your outcomes. That you aren't a victim of life, because **everyone** has some plight or disadvantage. She embodied independence and encouraged dusting yourself off quickly when you fell down. Some of the lessons she shared with me I wasn't capable of comprehending at that time, but still, they stayed with me, and I can't say I've ever had a superior who left such a lasting impression on my professional character as much.

Still, afterwards, I moved through the corporate world with lackluster success. I was probably a bit loud, people-pleasing, not detailed or organized enough, not professional enough, or just the right amount of meek to get pushed out or flat-out fired (and deservedly so).

At one point, I found myself making a good salary and going to 6-star restaurants. I'd wander the streets of Soho alone with flowers in my hand, watching people rush home to their loved ones, thinking, "I'm sad. Why do I get sad the minute I am alone?"

As I walked through life, it felt as though my hands and legs were pressed down close to my body while the only thing that moved freely were my eyes. I was watching the world while everything else felt rigid and weighed down. It felt like I lived in a box.

I think in 2021 it's easy to have the language to describe those feelings—a lack of a self defined identity, perfectionism etc... We can thank Instagram psychologist accounts for that. :-) However, at the time that was the best way I could describe my experience then.

DECIDING TO TURN IT INTO GOLD.

I was fired/laid off from every single job except for two, and decided to turn *ish into gold.

At that point, I realized I needed a therapist and started seeing the friendliest, prettiest one I could find. And she changed my life.

The greatest gift she gave to me was igniting my subdued desire to leave America. Within three months of her reminding me of this, I found myself on a plane to Japan, with a job offer and a fresh new life ahead. I fell in love a few times. Got sick. Traveled. Learned what being alone **really** meant and **deeply deeply** learned the value of money.

When I learned my dad's cancer was untreatable, I came back home. And a few weeks later, he died.

From there, I started interviewing and found myself starting another new life in San Francisco. But life has a way of always showing you your patterns. And so, that shiny new job, apartment and friendships? They didn't last. I was let go, again, and at that moment, I decided my heart couldn't handle another—self created —corporate disappointment again.

I committed to creating my company - my second actually, my first I started in Japan - and eventually made my way to my mother's guest room; after four months of miraculous bill paying including 3k in rent, moving costs and a shiny new 30k business mastermind agreement.

And it's in that room where I currently write this with a pack of sour cream Pringles, an Amanda Frances meditation playing, and my sovereign flower essence from faeryessence.com.

My business is almost three years old, and it's the reason why I'm alive.

BOOM. GOLD.

Now, I help people own their worth and go after the title and salary they deserve.

Honestly, I get it. My corporate working career reads like the most depressing story that never ends.

But because of that, it's effortless to relate to the clients that come to me. Generally speaking, they are all hardworking corporate professionals who need help with various aspects of the job search.

From burnt-out job seekers out of work for over a year, to GenZ'ers looking for career fulfillment, to badass millennial women dealing with sexual harassment work trauma, I've seen and been honored enough to assist with it all. Your work is your life—just like your relationships.

At SoulWork, we recognize how we're always creating our outcomes based on what we think we can have. And, because I've been in the job market quite a bit, I have experienced what social anxiety, people-pleasing, and imposter syndrome can do to your career. As a result, it's been easy to recognize those qualities in others and help them land someplace great despite it.

Having been out of work more often than not means I can teach you how to develop storytelling and interviewing skills. Coupled with having my first position basically be in sales (epic salary negotiation skills) and having an eye for knowing what recruiters, busy founders and HR teams want to see (hello, I am a whole recruiter!), I'm the best job search coach I know. And, I know a lot...

I'm also a minority and unfortunately, I have seen the differences that happen when companies hire—for example, an ESL candidate from France vs India. Ageism, discrimination and biases in the hiring process are real.

So, nothing makes me happier than seeing a quiet, soft-spoken hardworking badass interview into a role they **dreamed** about having and getting it with the **highest possible offer** they can.

Let's talk more about that, actually.
I'd love to end my chapter with a lesson. :-)
You're a SoulWork client now.
Let's start!

GOLD AS IN CASH MONEY.

So many people are afraid to be greedy. I don't think greediness is a bad thing, at least not anymore. Because if you're not greedy or self-interested first, who will be greedy for you? I've found most people will look after you, but it always helps to decide what you want, make sure no one 'loses' from it and then not let anyone talk you out of it.

Understand what salary you should want. And here's a hint: it's the highest possible for your function and years of experience possible. Ask for **that**. And don't back down.

I've hired and interviewed and seen so many (typically men) have the most audacious salary requirements with so little reason to back it up, except they want it. And I watched them get it. Be like those people.

While you're at it, you can still be a responsible participant in society. You can still be a team member. Be 'good'. Whatever you desire. But ask for what you want just like everyone else. Even if you grew up feeling like you didn't deserve it. And even if your voice shakes, and you feel hot all over and you have sweaty palms. ASK FOR IT ANYWAY.

How?

You do it by getting an advocate to remind you of your worth right before your interview or salary negotiation meeting. Additionally, you can be your own advocate by asking yourself:

- What's on the line for us (the you that's asking and the you that's listening - likely your inner child?
- What will take a back seat in your life if you don't push for it (ie. What have you given up in the past when you put the company first)?
- What are you giving up NOW by allowing them to talk you out of the 5K, 10K or 15K more you *really* want?
- Why SHOULD you take less? (Spoiler alert: you don't.)
- Why are you competent, and worthy of more? (Spoiler alert: everything about you - including the bits you have't loved and integrated into yourself yet.)

The best thing you can do for yourself is to grant yourself the grace to let the good in, even when it feels scary. It will in the beginning. And even if you mess up...don't be harsh to yourself any more especially when other people are just as human as you are.

It's okay to not know who you are at times.
It's okay to not feel great about being fired, laid off, pushed out.
It's okay to be disappointed or unhappy in your career.

But what's not okay is staying in places that make you feel this way. Allowing yourself to be the victim in a

negotiation or work situation. Assume that someone will rescue you.

Or keep beating yourself up.

Hiring a support team will aid you in getting the pay, the title and the self respect you've been waiting for because if you hire the right person they'll teach you how to get it from yourself first; which will enable the world to reflect it back to you. That's the best best best part. Because once you can get it from yourself, yes, it'll be nice when others reflect it back to you but it's even nicer once you realize it never goes away.

So.

The only difference between you and the folks that seem to get what they want is that they ask for it and surround themselves with people that remind them of it, and commit to deciding to receive.

Let's decide to have YOU play for this team then, shall we?
All the love, always,

Stephanie Heath
and the SoulWork & Six Figures team

ABOUT THE AUTHOR
STEPHANIE HEATH

Stephanie Heath (she/her) is a former Recruiter (Investment Banking, Amazon & Sony) and current Job Search, Career & Abundance Coach that helps soft-spoken men and women land and negotiate soul-aligned, six-figure, corporate positions. Her global online business, SoulWork & Six Figures, has transformed the lives of thousands of uninspired professionals by teaching them how to tap into their corporateWORTH, interview powerfully, and negotiate high six-figure salaries. Her work has been featured in Yahoo Finance, LinkedIn, Ontario News at Five, Well + Good and more, as well as in-person and online workshops; turning awkward interviewees into confident multiple offers earners around the globe. She is a native New Yorker born to Jamaican immigrant parents who loves Kundalini, animal friends and the sea.

Website: www.soulworkandselfies.com
Instagram:www.instagram.com/careercoachsteph/
Facebook Group: www.facebook.com/groups/SoulWorkandSixFigures

Additional: https://healerswanted.com/directory/stephanie-heath/
Linkedin: www.linkedin.com/in/stephanieheath/
Email: Hello@soulworkandselfies.com

25

TONI-ANN CAPECE

HONOR YOUR TRUTH

Young me would never know the power behind my vision. Lost in self-doubt, slowly being eaten away by questionable societal actions. An observer and passionate being, trying to understand the larger purpose in life. A dedicated young lady, wanting to perfect everything and solve all problems. Wearing my heart on my sleeve; expecting everyone will be treated with love, respect and dignity. Constantly questioning. Why do people choose to hurt others? Why do people choose to say hurtful words? I quickly learned to hold onto those people who inspire me to be a better person, treat me with respect, and bring joy into my life. I began to tighten my trust circle, removing people that chose to not uplift or inspire me to be a better person; I slowly eliminated added stress from my life. I noticed the obstacles my family was facing and focused on giving my love and energy to the people who have been by my side since I was born. I'm grateful to say that for me, those people are my loving-loud-loyal Italian and Hispanic family.

I come from a large immediate family: one brother, three sisters, two nephews, one niece, and grandparents on both sides. Growing up, it was more about the simple pleasures in life. I was raised in a small cape-style home in New Jersey and shared one bedroom with my two older sisters. This experience allowed us to have midnight dance parties while my parents thought we were sleeping and created the fun, trusting and loving sisterly connection we continue to have. After being the baby for sixteen years, my parents had my little sister. Helping to raise her sweet soul motivated me to set a good example of what a trusting, safe, and loving relationship feels like. I am dedicated to creating a safe space for her and future generations to heal, grow, and live a healthy purposeful life.

I have two amazing and extremely hardworking parents that didn't come from much. My father grew up in Brooklyn, NY where I spent a majority of my summers with my loving grandma, aunts, uncles, and cousins. My father dedicated his whole life to working hard to provide for his family to give us a better life than he had. Still to this day, he wakes up at 5am to catch the train to New York City, works a full day, finds time to work out, and eats dinner with the family each night. My financial awareness was heightened at a young age as I observed how hard my parents worked to build our life. My father instilled loyalty, trust, respect, and strong family values in demonstration of how to treat others. However, much of my father's side of the family did not share their emotions or heartache. There was an unspoken rule that family problems were kept private and never to be shared.

My mother balanced being a mom with being a hardworking leader to show her children the importance of being a strong independent woman. Mami Chiqui, my grandmother, always told us to never rely on anyone for our own success or happiness. My mother shared values of aspiration, always telling me to dream big and reach my goals. Being born and raised in Guatemala and coming to the United States at age eleven had once been a dream for her; she reached it, and more!

My love for helping others started with my family. In middle school, I motivated my father to quit smoking cigarettes and to lose sixty pounds for health reasons. I remember our first day working out together, I took him to Tamaques Park in New Jersey. We started by walking, then jogging, and over time my father would sprint past me in the park. Still to this day, the feeling I get when we go for a run and he laps me is indescribable. It feels good to support someone else and in turn strengthen a relationship. The commitment my father currently has to his physical health, financial success, and family happiness inspires me daily.

THE TRUTH COMES OUT

When I think about my childhood experiences, I consider myself someone with secondary trauma. Living in a chaotic household trying to understand and support others around me. I noticed my mother was a strong woman who struggled to receive love from my compassionate father due to her anxiety, discomfort, and depression from past lived experiences. Prior to marrying my father, my mother had a difficult past. She describes my father as her saving grace. My mother's previous relationships and life experiences affect how she copes with everyday stressors.

As a young lady, I learned I was being raised by a resilient mother who experienced multiple cases of sexual abuse and domestic violence as a young girl. Growing up, this was difficult to understand, yet I was passionate about supporting my mother. I saw myself as a vessel to support others who have been through traumatic events, to get them to a place of healing and self-acceptance.

My mother shared her experiences with me to inform the reality and power of human beings. She demonstrated that you can break free from the cycle of abuse and trauma. She raised me to be independent, and always supported and trusted my decisions. She reminded me to trust my gut instinct and that she is here for me no matter what obstacle I face. Her actions continue to always speak louder than her words. She demonstrated true unconditional love, and I honor her for those teachings. Although she wanted to hide from her truth, she knew that she needed to share her story to try to protect her children from possibly experiencing her truth. My mother's experiences allowed her to be vulnerable, to share herself and love entirely with her kids. To show that she is not perfect. To ensure that we know our worth and what unconditional love truly feels like. I am grateful for my resilient mother who has been vulnerable enough to share her experiences with me; to share the depth behind human beings, and remind me that we never know the path someone has walked.

Another impactful moment in my life was when my brother returned home from serving overseas in Afghanistan and Iraq. He was faced with quickly adjusting back to civilian life, being away from his Marine family, and healing from platoon brothers who committed suicide. High anxiety led to panic attacks, all while having to work through starting the next chapter in his life. At that time, I saw how critical the need for family love and support is.

According to the American Psychiatric Association, Posttraumatic Stress Disorder (PTSD) is a psychiatric disorder that millions of people face due to experiencing or witnessing a traumatic event like: war/combat, sexual violence, domestic violence, a serious accident, natural disaster, or being threatened with death. People with PTSD have penetrating, unsettling thoughts and feelings related to their traumatic experience that remain with them after the event has passed. Flashbacks or nightmares may occur, creating a feeling of detachment from your body and a sense of separation from other people.

What may be lesser known is secondary trauma; this can be experienced by a person who had indirect exposure to a traumatic event, and has been affected by someone else's experience and suffering. The individual has taken on the emotional stress to support someone in overcoming their experience. My experiences in coping with secondary trauma have turned me into the non-judgmental, anxiety-driven, humble, sensitive, loving person that I am today. I have been guided here to create safe connections for people to heal and feel confident in sharing their truth, and to create more meaningful and impactful relationships within our communities. At a young age, I learned to let go of the small troubles and think big. I encourage you to think about the importance of life, your legacy, and the impact you want to make on the world for future generations to follow.

ACCEPTING YOUR TRUTH

Are you running away from your inner truth and fears? Yogis talk a lot about healing inner trauma...but what does that mean or look like? The more people learn about themselves, the more they will understand how their experiences affect their being. People may experience the same situation but respond differently to the event.

Let's consider an individual with a strong support system and minimal personal and professional stressors who is seeking professional help; as compared to an individual faced with the same traumatic experience, however without a trusted person to rely on, while dealing with job loss and being evicted from their apartment. The way the person reacts and copes to the situation will vary tremendously on current social, environmental, and psychological factors. When taking a trauma-sensitive approach to support survivors, it's important to never compare human experiences because everyone's response to a situation is unique. This means the approach we take to heal is also very unique.

Our character might come out in different ways when under pressure: crying, anger, laughter, anxiety, fear, destruction, and so on. Why do feelings present themselves and arise at the most unexpected moments? The answer is because those traumatic experiences were never faced. You may have discussed the situation, but have you accepted it? Accepting your truth is not about understanding why you experienced an event, but understanding you are strong and resilient enough to cope with the difficult experience and create behavioral changes to move past the experience. It's about leaning on your support system to get you through a difficult time in life. If you continue to ask yourself, "Why me? What did I do to deserve this?" you will never find a good head space to accept the truth. Accepting the events that have occurred in your life will give you the motivation to see the light past the pain.

When you begin to ask, "Am I going to be alright?" take time to consider who is in your trust circle. Lean into your support system and utilize community resources. Begin to lean into the pain and know that your past does not define you. Trust that everyone has the power to succeed past their trauma or personal experiences.

Most people struggle with controlling their nervous system and begin to become disconnected from their body. The reason emotional and physical feelings arise is because the underlying problem has not been tackled. As human beings, we make up a meaning and interpretation to our own event and continue to recreate the fear in our heads. We struggle with breaking away from how we respond to an event, because it feels safe. It could be a traumatic event that occurred when we were a child; it could even be something like kids bullying you in school or your parents picking you up late. These fears end up manifesting and become the way you react and respond to similar situations. For example, Paul cheated. Your body immediately feels anxiety, fear, and shuts down because you are in shock. Your nervous system generalizes your reaction and says, "All men are cheaters," to keep you safe. However, a person with no emotional response would distinguish just Paul as a cheater. The procrastination, perfectionism, confusion, feel of failure, and distraction are all appropriate responses to trauma that has not healed.

I challenge you to reflect on your legacy and question how you respond to life events when under pressure. Begin to reflect on underlying trauma and determine the meaning behind your emotional and physical reactions.

FACING TRAUMA .

For some people with severe PTSD, high anxiety can last several days. My brother explained, "I'd be at a restaurant and go into a panic attack. It was embarrassing. You can't think, your head gets foggy, and you can't even talk. My mood is off and nothing feels right."

Learning to cope with personal experiences is a lifelong practice. Assess your social, environmental, and psychological factors and how they impact your mental health. The lifestyle a person lives and functions within can play a major role in mental health. You will feel the best when you consistently practice emotion-based coping skills to guide you through your healing journey. Some emotion-based coping skills are: yoga, aromatherapy, journaling, meditation, taking a walk, listening or playing music, reading a book, painting. It's important to also stay physically healthy by drinking water, moving your body, and getting ample sleep. The power behind controlling anxiety, fear, or stress is in managing your mental and physical state. It is an ongoing practice that instills clarity to support you in identifying and releasing your emotions.

Practicing mindfulness is one approach toward releasing emotional distress to begin creating behavioral change. Healing begins once you create a place of safety within your body. Start by acknowledging the sensations that arise and notice the occurring emotional patterns happening inside of you. As emotions heighten, begin to analyze the way you behave, feel, and think. Assess how you feel moving recurring thoughts from a place of discomfort to a place of positivity and light. Reducing anxiety is about reframing your state of mind.

Through meditation and somatic experiencing, I use a trauma-sensitive approach to discuss the behaviors or emotions that arise. I guide clients through releasing locked emotions to feel comfortable in channeling their feelings. We work to identify barriers and take steps to change actions associated with past life experiences to create behavioral change.

Facing your truth is the consciousness of understanding the root cause of your behaviors. Throughout your healing process, become an observer and focus on reaching a state of awareness. The more you receive clarity, understand emotional patterns and face your truth, the more you will feel confident in expressing your authentic self. Trust that emotional patterns will fade and behaviors will change if you put in the time and energy to heal.

Be aware of your state of mind. Determining when you are not in the right state of mind does not mean you are weak. It means you have a lot going on in your everyday life and need time to slow it down. Attract people in your life who care to learn about you and your experiences. Having a support system that accepts you and your legacy is crucial. It's about surrounding yourself around people who make you feel comfortable in those uncomfortable situations. If you need to leave the bar, they say, "Let's go," no questions asked. That's how you know who your real friends are. It's the special people who take time to understand your triggers and not use them against you, but instead to support you.

Trust that your story does not define you and you can overcome any life challenge. I am here to be a vessel of safety, courage, hope, and release. Know there is a community of healers, right here, that also feel fear, guilt, and shame. The more we share our story and personal experiences, the more we can create meaningful relationships with others and foster a space that everyone feels safe living in. But first, it's important to create that meaningful relationship with your own body. Love yourself. Accept that your experiences do not resemble your values or beliefs. In fact, your life experiences may challenge you to discover new values or beliefs that connect with your heart and life purpose.

The ingredient you need to change an area in your life is dedication. Can you keep a promise to actively work on healing yourself? I challenge you to utilize the tools and resources in this book to better connect with your legacy. Honor yourself and the truth behind who you are. Change starts with you and YOU are worth it!

WHAT CAN YOU DO?

I encourage you to begin by being a non-judgmental ear to your friends, family, and others in your community. I encourage you to find opportunities to create environments of safety, to have meaningful conversations, and foster communities of belonging. I believe that is the greatest way to leave your mark on the world. If you notice someone is alone or on edge, check in and see what's on their mind, rather than reacting or questioning their behavior. Remember that you never walked a day in anyone's shoes and have no clue what others may be experiencing. Take time to understand your friends' triggers, to not use it against them, but to support them and strengthen your relationship. The more you begin to be a friend that asks vulnerable questions, the more you will understand the depth behind humanity and the work needed to heal our legacy and future generations to come.

I share my story so that survivors know they are not alone. That anyone can move past traumatic experiences to live a life free from fear and anxiety. To break free from emotional and physical barriers that impact the ability to live a more purpose-driven life. To be able to build trusting relationships and find safety within our bodies to ultimately create a life filled with joy, love and connection with others. I believe you are reading my story for a reason, and trust you will take this sensitive information with you to better connect with yourself and create a safe place for others to heal and grow.

ABOUT THE AUTHOR

TONI-ANN CAPECE

Toni-Ann Capece is a Social Worker, Trauma-Informed Yoga Therapist, and Sexual Assault Advocate. Toni-Ann elevates the voices of individuals who have experienced traumatic events and have overcome life challenges. She teaches the philosophy of yoga through the lens of social work to provide a holistic, trauma-sensitive approach that stimulates personal growth. Toni-Ann supports individuals in recognizing and regulating sensations that arise in the body. She works to calm the body to support individuals in releasing stress and regain a feeling of safety inside their body.

Toni-Ann's vision is to guide healers in embracing their energy through physical, mental, and spiritual practices. Her mission is to encourage healthy living and coping skills through yoga movement and meditation. Toni-Ann is grateful to share her yoga practice to help others release negative energies, recognize the impacts of trauma, understand how it affects the ability to feel love, joy, and satisfaction.

Instagram: www.instagram.com/toniiann.c/
Instagram: www.instagram.com/theeamethysttree/
Email: theeamethysttree@gmail.com

26

ABOUT EXALTED PUBLISHING HOUSE AND BRIDGET AILEEN SICSKO

Since I was young, I knew I was here to help people. Why? How? When? I had a lot of questions. But as life tends to do so, the path seamlessly unfolded in front of me. Not quite in the ways one would expect it to, but ah that is life, right?

Let's take a trip down memory lane. Age fifteen. I was a normal suburban New Jersey girl with a love for sports, hiking, working out, and hanging with my friends. But I also was struggling inside. Parasites, frequent pneumonia, rapid weight loss, colitis, and staph infections riddled my body as a result of Lymes disease. Feeling frustrated after going to doctor after doctor with no answers, I set out on a quest—one that I didn't realize at the time would impact the entire trajectory of my life.

As I look back and make sense of this pivotal moment on my journey, I realized something. Sitting in a gastroenterology office, my purpose fell into my lap.

I had brought all of my medical records—diagnoses, antibiotics, treatments and protocols—since I had begun to connect the dots that everything in the body is connected through studying Ayurveda and holistic health. He didn't even look at the folder that I had spent hours compiling.

Here was my purpose—to *never* ever let someone go through life feeling unseen or unheard ever again and broadcast these messages as far and wide as possible.
To make sure that all voices were heard.
To honor people's experiences and never write them off.
To really listen to people.
And to share the stories that aren't being shared.

Fast forward to now, I have the pleasure of working daily with entrepreneurs who have a big mission on this planet. They are coaches, entrepreneurs, healers, yogis, teachers, consultants, and advisors who are all here to help humans evolve into the higher version of themselves, whether it be business, health, or purpose.

What I am dedicated to at this point in my journey is to continue to share powerful stories.
To remind you that your voice matters.
No matter where you are on your personal journey, your voice matters.
No matter what you have faced or experienced, your voice matters.

Here's to the voice revolution—one of most pivotal pieces of my own Legacy.

Cheers to Legacy Speaks.

Bridget Aileen Sicsko is the founder of Exalted Publishing House, a Podcast Host and Sales & Messaging Coach. She helps successful entrepreneurs standout and be featured as a leader in their industry through sharing powerful stories. Her mission is to amplify the voices of powerful entrepreneurs who are ready to elevate their business, become published authors & public speakers. Bridget also hosts a live interview series called "The Gathering MVMT" where she has interviewed over 40 entrepreneurs, TedX speakers, authors, thought-leaders, & visionaries who are here to uplift humanity. She lives in New Jersey with her husband and border collie-beagle, Finn.

Exalted Publishing House

Made in the USA
Las Vegas, NV
29 May 2023

72703482R00157